First published in Great Britain in 2019 by

SLC Tuition LTD

www.SLCtuition.co.uk

Copyright © Sarah Louise Chauhan 2019

Sarah Louise Chauhan has asserted her right under the Copyright, Designs and Patents Act 1988 to be identified as the author of this work.

All rights reserved. No part of this publication may be reproduced, stored in a retrieval system or transmitted, in any form or by any other means, without the publisher's prior permission in writing.

This book is sold subject to the condition that it shall not, by way of trade or otherwise, be lent, resold, hired out or otherwise circulated without the publisher's prior consent in any form of binding or cover other than in that which it is published and without a similar condition, including this condition, being imposed on the subsequent purchaser.

Every reasonable effort has been made to trace copyright holders of material reproduced in this book, but if any have been inadvertently overlooked the publishers would be glad to hear from them.

© Sarah Louise Chauhan 2019 – *copying, sharing or unauthorised distribution of this document in part or whole in any public arena including online is strictly prohibited. Action will be taken against any companies, organisations or individuals found to be in breach of these rules.*

Contents

How to use this book – Information for parents – Page 3

Introduction to algebra – Page 4

Lesson 1: Algebra basics – Page 5

Lesson 2: Creating simple equations – Page 12

Lesson 3: Using simple equations to calculate things – Page 17

Lesson 4: Rearranging equations to change the variable – Page 21

Lesson 5: Rearranging equations to find the solution – Page 25

Lesson 6: Suggesting values for missing numbers – Page 29

Lesson 7: Solving complex word problems by forming equations – Page 33

Lesson 8: End of topic assessment – Page 37

Answers to exercises – Page 43

© Sarah Louise Chauhan 2019 – *copying, sharing or unauthorised distribution of this document in part or whole in any public arena including online is strictly prohibited. Action will be taken against any companies, organisations or individuals found to be in breach of these rules.*

How to use this book – information for parents.

This book is arranged into a series of 8 lessons each which will enable you to teach your child algebra in preparation for their 11+ or KS2 SATS exams.

Each week your child should study one lesson and the worked examples contained within that lesson. At the end of each week's lesson there is a set of questions based on the Book Objective covered in that lesson. Your child's ability to complete these questions successfully will tell you how much of that lesson they have absorbed and will identify any areas of weakness. Whilst completing the exercises it is not necessary to time your child. It is more important that your child has time to complete the questions correctly.

It is key to your child's success that they actively review the questions that they did not answer correctly. The ability and willingness of your child to go back over questions or concepts that they did not fully understand will differentiate them as an excellent student as opposed to an average one.

The last lesson in this book consists of an end of topic assessment. In this assessment you will find questions to test your child's knowledge of everything in this book. The worked answers to both the lesson exercises and end of topic tests are to be found at the end of the book and will allow you to correctly mark your child's work. These answers will also allow you to guide your child on where they have gone wrong, should they have answered a question incorrectly. There is a suggested time limit of 50 minutes for the End of Topic assessment, it is not absolutely necessary for you to adhere to this time limit however, learning to work under time pressure is a key skill which all students will need to master in time for their formal assessments.

Finally, the importance of rest, good nutrition and an adequate amount of leisure time cannot be underrated. The years leading up to child's 11+ or SATS exams can be stressful and the best results always come from students who work hard but also sleep well, eat well and have free time to let their minds wander away from exam preparations.

I hope you and your child find Algebra Booster useful and wish you the best of luck on your 11+ or SATS journey!

© Sarah Louise Chauhan 2019 – *copying, sharing or unauthorised distribution of this document in part or whole in any public arena including online is strictly prohibited. Action will be taken against any companies, organisations or individuals found to be in breach of these rules.*

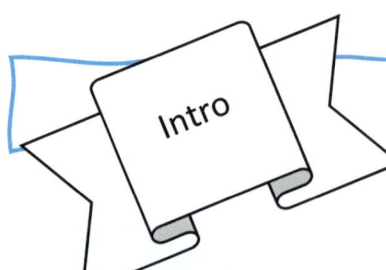

ALGEBRA

Book Objectives:

By the end of this book you should be able to:

1) Understand the basics of algebra.
2) Form your own simple equations.
3) Use simple equations to calculate things.
4) Rearrange equations to change the variable.
5) Rearrange equations to find the solution.
6) Suggest values for missing numbers where there is more than one variable.
7) Solve complex word problems by forming equations.

What is algebra?

Algebra is a way of doing maths where you replace numbers with letters or symbols. Algebra allows us to create equations that can then enable us to calculate things. For example; Albert Einstein's most famous equation $E=mc^2$ allows us to calculate the amount of energy stored in an object if we know its mass. Or Newton's $F = (Gm_1m_2)/r^2$ will allow us to calculate the force of gravity between the Earth and the Sun.

These equations were world changing and are far more complicated than anything you will tackle in preparation for your 11+ or SATS exam. However, by learning algebra you will be gaining the knowledge which may one day enable you to create ground-breaking equations and become a famous scientist!

© Sarah Louise Chauhan 2019 – *copying, sharing or unauthorised distribution of this document in part or whole in any public arena including online is strictly prohibited. Action will be taken against any companies, organisations or individuals found to be in breach of these rules.*

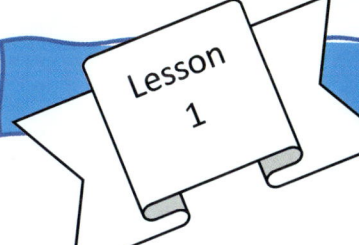

Algebra basics.

Algebra is all about using symbols and letters to make calculations shorter. Imagine that I am planning a surprise birthday party for my grandad. I could write the following word equation to represent how many people are being invited in total:

Total number of guests = No. of school friends + No. of family memebers + No. of work friends

As you can see, this has become quite a large word equation and has taken up a lot of space. To make this equation shorter and more sensible we can replace the individual phrases with symbols or letters.

$T = $ Total number of guests invited

$S = $ No. of old school friends

$B = $ No. of family members

$F = $ No. of work friends

Using these letters as substitutes for the original phrases I can now rewrite my equation as:

$T = S + B + F$

This equation means the same thing as my original word equation but is now shorter and looks more sensible.

It is important to note that it doesn't matter what symbol or letters you pick to use when creating equations. (As long as you don't use the same symbol or letter twice for different things).

Brackets.

When looking at an equation brackets help us to see what needs to happen first.

For example:

$(x + 2) - 4$

This equation tells us that x and 2 must be added together first, before 4 is subtracted from the total.

In algebra BODMAS still applies.

Multiplication.

In algebra we NEVER use the x symbol to multiply things together. Instead we just put the two or more things that need to be multiplied next to each other.

For example:

xyz

This equation tells us to multiply x by y by z.

Division.

In algebra we NEVER use the ÷ symbol to divide things. Instead we put the thing that needs to be divided on the top of the thing that it's being divided by.

For example:

$$\frac{x}{2}$$

This equation tells us to divide x by 2.

© Sarah Louise Chauhan 2019 – *copying, sharing or unauthorised distribution of this document in part or whole in any public arena including online is strictly prohibited. Action will be taken against any companies, organisations or individuals found to be in breach of these rules.*

Simplifying equations.

Sometimes we can encounter equations which can be made simpler. We can either simplify by adding, subtracting, multiplying or dividing **like terms**.

Like terms are parts of an equation that are the same. For example; $4e$, e, $9e$ and $2e$ are all like terms as they are all different amounts of e.

When collecting like terms you must be careful as sometimes things which look alike are not the same. For example; $4e$ and $9e^2$ are not the same as one is e and the other one is e^2.

$4e + 3e + e - 2e = 6e$

Here all the $e's$ can be collected together by either adding or subtracting them.

$4e + 2f + e - f = 5e + f$

In this example both the $e's$ and $f's$ can be collected separately.

$$\frac{6e}{2} = 3e$$

In this example the numbers are like terms and so can be divided as usual to give 3.

$4e(5e) = 20e^2$

In this example we are being asked to multiply $4e$ by $5e$. As 4 and 5 are like terms (they are both numbers) they get multiplied to make 20. As e and e are like terms they get multiplied to give e^2.

$2e(4e - 5) = 8e^2 - 10e$

Here everything inside the brackets is to be multiplied by $2e$. Once the multiplication has taken place the equation cannot be simplified any further because e^2 and e are not like terms.

$-2e - 9b - 4e + 2b = -6e - 7b$

Here the $e's$ and $b's$ can be collected together separately to simplify the equation.

© Sarah Louise Chauhan 2019 – *copying, sharing or unauthorised distribution of this document in part or whole in any public arena including online is strictly prohibited. Action will be taken against any companies, organisations or individuals found to be in breach of these rules.*

Worked example 1.

📄 Sally begins with several sweets, the number of sweets she has changes as different things happen.

Create equations to show how many sweet Sally will end up with. Use the following symbols in your equations:

$y =$ number of sweets that Sally begins with.

$x =$ number of sweets that Sally has at the end.

Scenario	Answer	Notes
Sally gives away three sweets to her little sister.	$x = y - 3$	
Sally is given 10 more sweets by her mom.	$x = y + 10$	
Sally halves the number of sweets she has by giving half to her best friend Sanjana.	$x = \dfrac{y}{2}$	In algebra we never use the ÷ symbol instead we write divisions like fractions with the number that is being divided on the top and the number that it is being divided by on the bottom.
Sally doubles the number of sweets she has by winning a game of chess against her classmate Rajiv.	$x = 2y$	In algebra we never use the x symbol to multiply two things together. Instead we just put the two things that are to be multiplied next to each other. So, 2 multiplied by y is 2y.
Sally squares the number of sweets she has by coming 2nd in her school's maths Olympiad.	$x = y^2$	
Sally loses half of her sweets in a game of chess but then wins back 7 sweets in the following game.	$x = \left(\dfrac{y}{2}\right) + 7$	The brackets are necessary as they show that the starting number of sweets must be halved before 7 sweets are added afterwards.
Sally gives away 12 of her sweets to her friend who fell over and then loses half of the remaining amount in a game of backgammon.	$x = \dfrac{(y - 12)}{2}$	The brackets are again necessary as they show that 12 sweets must be removed from the starting amount before the remaining amount is halved.
Sally is given 4 sweets by her teacher as she gained top marks in her maths test. Sally's mom then squares the number of sweets as a reward for being such a hardworking daughter.	$x = (y + 4)^2$	Here the brackets show that 4 sweets must be added to Sally's starting amount before the number of sweets she has is squared.

Page | 7

© Sarah Louise Chauhan 2019 – *copying, sharing or unauthorised distribution of this document in part or whole in any public arena including online is strictly prohibited. Action will be taken against any companies, organisations or individuals found to be in breach of these rules.*

Worked example 2.

A bottle of water costs x pence and a chocolate bar costs y pence.

Match each statement to the correct equation for the amount in pence.

The total cost of 3 bottles of water.	$700 - 2x$
The total cost of 8 bottles of water and 3 bars of chocolate.	$8x + 3y$
The total cost of 9 bottles of water and 9 bars of chocolate.	$3x$
The change from £7 when buying 2 bottles of water.	$9(x + y)$
Half of the cost of 7 bottles of water and 10 chocolate bars.	$\dfrac{(7x + 10y)}{2}$

Matches:
- The total cost of 3 bottles of water → $3x$
- The total cost of 8 bottles of water and 3 bars of chocolate → $8x + 3y$
- The total cost of 9 bottles of water and 9 bars of chocolate → $9(x + y)$
- The change from £7 when buying 2 bottles of water → $700 - 2x$
- Half of the cost of 7 bottles of water and 10 chocolate bars → $\dfrac{(7x + 10y)}{2}$

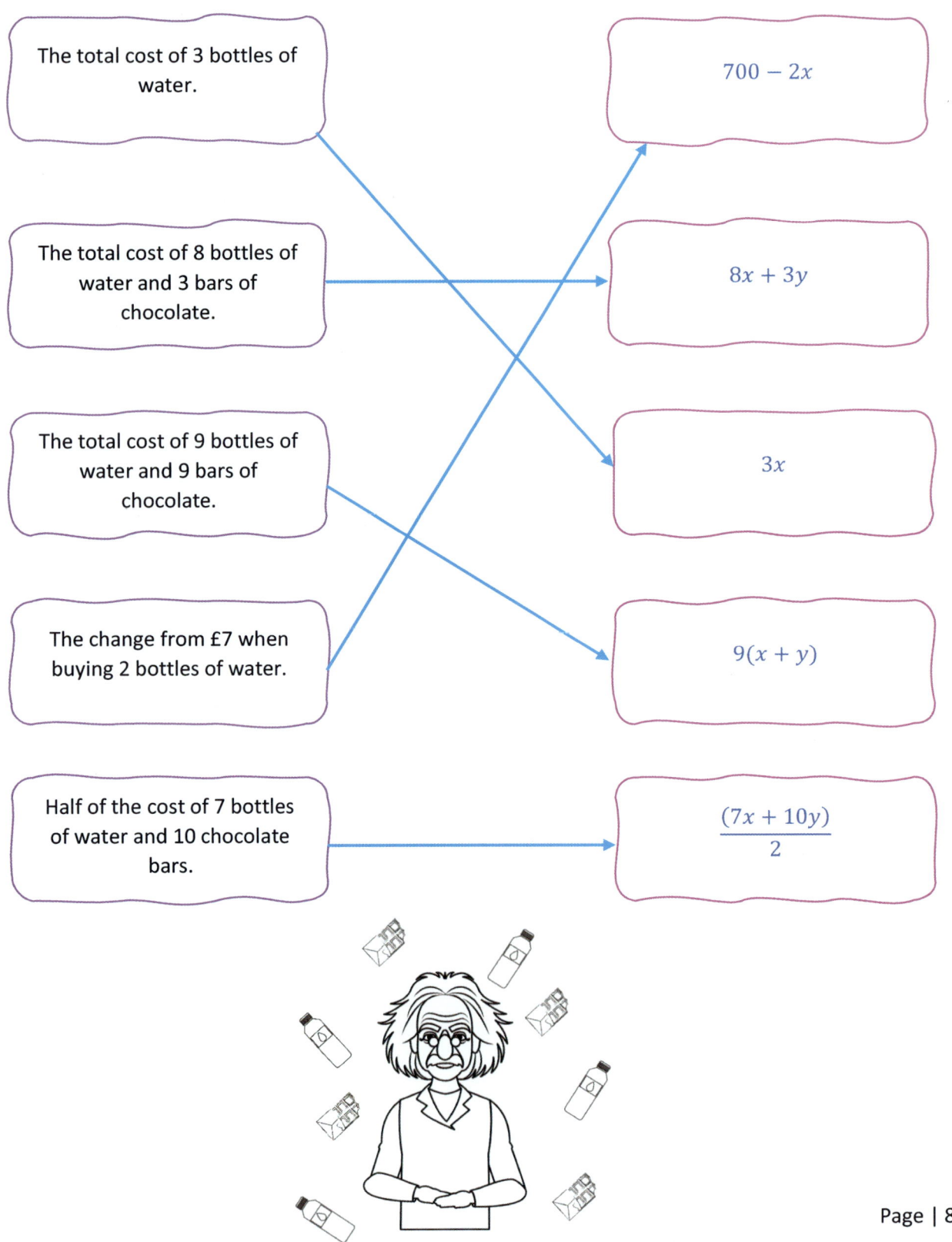

Exercise 1.

This exercise will test your knowledge of Book Objective 1. Use the worked answer booklet to check your answers. You will find extra questions for all of the Book Objectives in the end of topic test.

1) Match each statement to the correct equation.

Divide h by 2 and then add 5	h^2
Add 5 to h then divide the total by 2	$7h$
Square h	$\left(\dfrac{h}{2}\right) + 5$
Add 10 to h	$h + 10$
Subtract the square root of h from 7	$\dfrac{(h+5)}{2}$
Multiply h by 7.	$7 - \sqrt{h}$

© Sarah Louise Chauhan 2019 – *copying, sharing or unauthorised distribution of this document in part or whole in any public arena including online is strictly prohibited. Action will be taken against any companies, organisations or individuals found to be in breach of these rules.*

2) Match each equation on the left with the equivalent expression on the right.

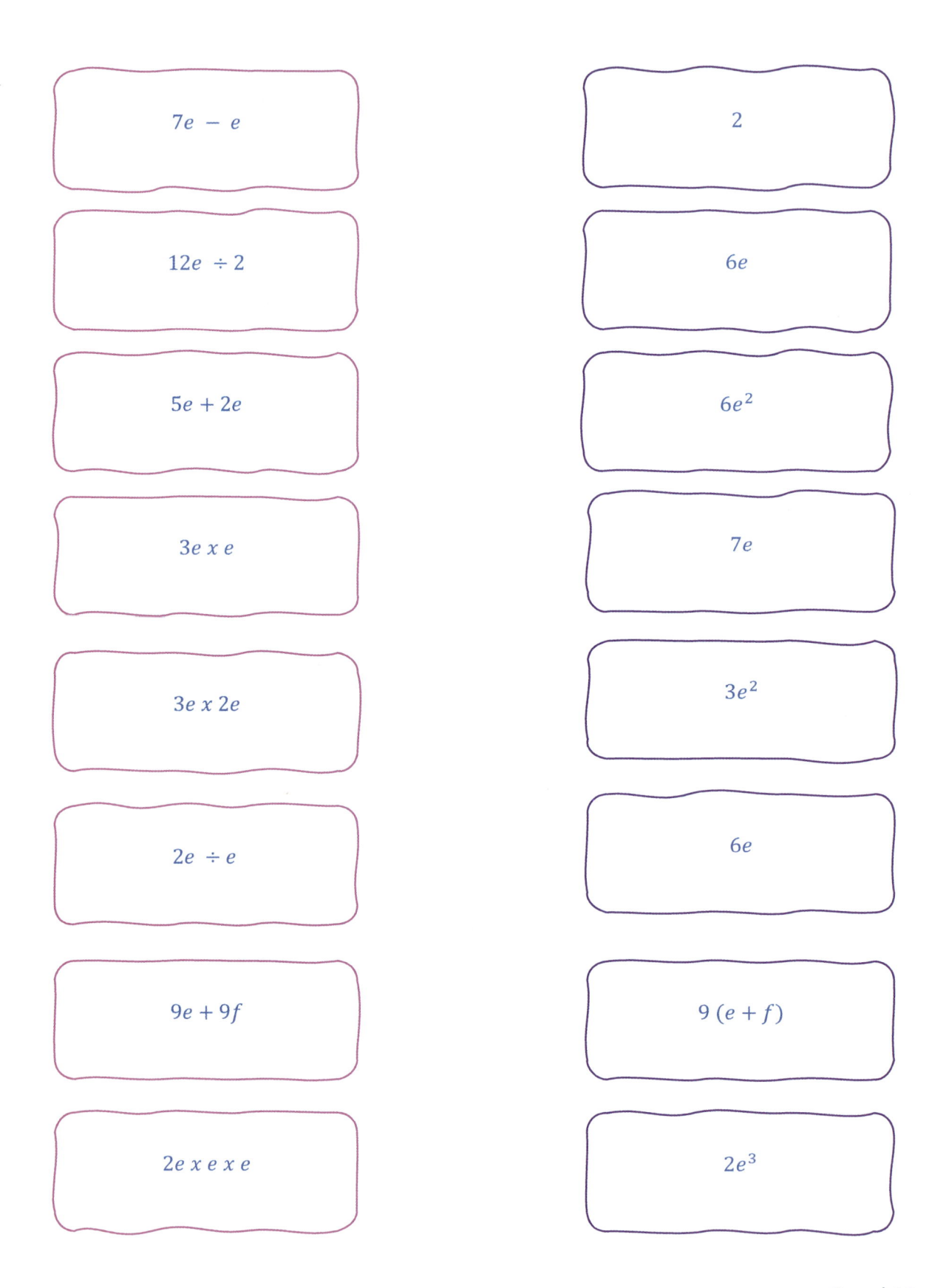

$7e - e$	2
$12e \div 2$	$6e$
$5e + 2e$	$6e^2$
$3e \times e$	$7e$
$3e \times 2e$	$3e^2$
$2e \div e$	$6e$
$9e + 9f$	$9(e + f)$
$2e \times e \times e$	$2e^3$

3) A pencil costs k pence, an eraser costs t pence and a sharpener costs m pence.

Match each statement to the correct equation for the amount in pence.

The total cost of 3 pencils, 3 erasers and 3 sharpeners.	$1000 - (12k + 3t)$
The cost of 6 pencils, three erasers and 12 sharpeners to be divided by 3 friends.	$\dfrac{(50k + 35t + 23m)}{2}$
The change from £10 when buying 12 pencils and 3 erasers.	$3(k + t + m)$
Half the cost of 50 pencils, 35 erasers and 23 sharpeners.	$4k$
One quarter of the cost of 16 pencils.	$2k + t + 4m$

Your score: ☐/19

Write your score for Exercise 1 here:

☛ **Remember** it is important that if you made any mistakes you go back and look at the question again. Even if you only got one question wrong the key to exam success is *learning from your mistakes*.

Lesson 2: Creating simple equations.

Imagine I want to calculate the cost of my shopping. When I go to the supermarket, I only buy apples and bananas (I have a very boring diet). The apples cost 45p and the bananas cost 30p each. We could write the following equation to calculate the total cost of my shopping:

Total cost of shopping = (45p x number of apples) + (30p x number of bananas)

However, this is looks too long.

The idea with algebra is we want to cut down the amount of words we use.

We could replace the phrase 'number of apples' with the letter A, and the phrase 'number of oranges' with the letter B. We will also replace the phrase 'Total cost of shopping' with the letter T. Our equation now looks like this:

$T = 45A + 30B$

> **Remember!** The brackets are there to show you the order in which you should do the calculation.

> **Important!** When we put numbers and letters next to each other in equations we don't need a multiplication sign. For example, 45A means 45 x A and AB means A x B.

Worked example 1.

Let's look at another example. Imagine I have a bathroom which I want to tile. The dimensions of the bathroom floor are shown below.

I want to create a formula for the area (A) of the bathroom floor so that I know how many tiles to buy.

(Diagram: rectangle with width 4Y and height 2Y)

Step 1: Our first step is to write a word equation for what we want to find.

Area = Length x Width

Step 2: We then add in the expressions or symbols that we have for the width and the height.

$A = 4Y \times 2Y$

Step 3: Now we must simplify the equation. We know that we need to remove the multiplication sign and we can also tidy the formula up by multiplying the like terms. The numbers 4 and 2 are like terms as they are both numbers so we can simplify them as 4 x 2 = 8.

The Y's are also like terms so $Y \times Y = Y^2$. Therefore, overall our expression becomes:

$A = 8Y^2$

© Sarah Louise Chauhan 2019 – *copying, sharing or unauthorised distribution of this document in part or whole in any public arena including online is strictly prohibited. Action will be taken against any companies, organisations or individuals found to be in breach of these rules.*

Worked example 2.

📄 **Rachel and Joey are planning to put decking in the corner of their garden. The diagram of the garden is below:**

Create an equation to give the area of the ground that they want to put decking on.

Step 1: Our first step is to write a word equation for what we want to find.

$$Area\ of\ a\ triangle = \frac{1}{2} \times base \times height$$

Step 2: We then add in the expressions or symbols that we have for the base and the height.

$$Area\ of\ a\ triangle = \frac{1}{2} \times (5x + 2) \times (2x)$$

Step 3: Now we must simplify the equation. To make this easier it is best to multiply $(5x + 2)$ by $(2x)$ first and then multiply by $\frac{1}{2}$.

$$Area\ of\ a\ triangle = \frac{1}{2} \times (5x + 2) \times (2x)$$

Make sure when multiplying $(5x + 2)$ by $(2x)$ you multiply both $5x$ and 2 by $2x$.

$$Area\ of\ a\ triangle = \frac{1}{2} \times (10x^2 + 4x)$$

$$Area\ of\ a\ triangle = 5x^2 + 2x$$

Worked example 3.

📄 **Danni and her dad have started a small business growing and selling roses. They begin with a certain number of roses which they quickly sell half to the wholesaler. From the remaining number of roses they manage to sell 20 at the 'FloralGB' exhibition. The remaining roses they will send to their local garden centre.**

Create an equation to show how many roses will be availble to sell at the gared centre. You should use the following symbols in your eqution:

$L = No.of\ roses\ remaining\ for\ sale\ at\ the\ garden\ centre.$

$B = No.of\ roses\ to\ begin\ with.$

Step 1: Our first step is to write a word equation for what we want to find.

$$No.of\ roses\ remaining\ for\ sale\ at\ garden\ centre = \left(\frac{No.of\ roses\ to\ begin\ with}{2}\right) - 20$$

Remember the brackets are there to show what part of the equation should be done first. Here the number of roses to begin with is halved when some are sold to the wholesaler. This happens BEFORE 20 are sold at 'FloralGB'.

Step 2: We then add in the expressions or symbols that we have. This gives us the following equation:

$$L = \left(\frac{B}{2}\right) - 20$$

Exercise 2.

This exercise will test your knowledge of Book Objective 2. Use the worked answer booklet to check your answers. You will find extra questions for all of the Book Objectives in the end of topic test.

1) Andy and his best friend Tariq are buying stock for the school tuck shop which they run. They buy crisps, chocolates and apples in different amounts each week. Create and equation to find out how many items they will buy, in total, each week. You should use the following symbols for your equation:
$T = Total\ items$
$R = Crisps$
$Y = Chocolate$
$A = Apples$

2) Susanne and Tyrone have some Rabbits for sale. They sell three of them. Create an equation to find out how many Rabbits they have left available. You should use the following symbols for your equation:
$L = Rabbits\ left\ available$
$S = Rabbits\ for\ sale\ at\ the\ beginning$

3) Amal has some books. She sells half of them and then buys another 20 to add to her stock. Create an equation to find out how many books she now has. You should use the following symbols for your equation:
$B = Number\ of\ books\ available\ at\ the\ beginning$
$E = Number\ of\ books\ available\ now$

4) A group of school students go on a school trip. There are 7 minibuses and 4 cars carrying the students to their destination. Create an equation to find out how many students go on the trip in total. You should use the following symbols in your equation:
$S = Total\ number\ of\ students$
$M = Number\ of\ students\ in\ each\ minibus$
$C = Number\ of\ students\ in\ each\ car$

5) Abigail has collected some Tadpoles from her pond at home and taken them to school for the Year 5 fish tank. Unfortunately, 5 of the Tadpoles get eaten by a hungry fish. Then the remaining number of Tadpoles gets halved as Abigail gives half of the remaining Tadpoles to the Year 4's for their fish tank. Create an equation to find the remaining number of Tadpoles.
$E = Number\ of\ Tadpoles\ at\ the\ end$
$S = Number\ of\ Tadpoles\ at\ the\ start$

6) Dion is helping his dad put a fence around their garden. The shape of the garden is shown below with the lengths of the sides given also. Create an equation to find the perimeter of the garden. You should use the following symbol in your equation, along with the sides given:
$P = Perimeter$

5D
4T

© Sarah Louise Chauhan 2019 – *copying, sharing or unauthorised distribution of this document in part or whole in any public arena including online is strictly prohibited. Action will be taken against any companies, organisations or individuals found to be in breach of these rules.*

7) Dion and his dad then decide to start carpeting their living room. The shape of their living room is shown with the lengths of the sides given. Create an equation to find the area of the living room.
You should use the following symbol in your equation, along with the sides given:
$A = Area\ of\ living\ room$

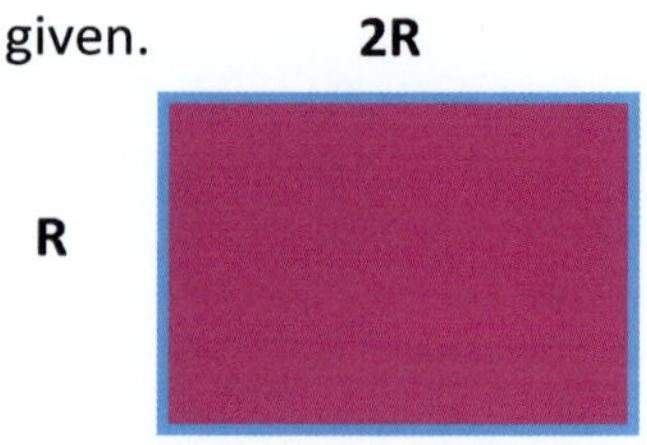

8) Anton is an architect. He has been asked to calculate the volume of a swimming pool in one of his client's homes as they want to fill the pool in with concrete. The shape of the pool is shown below. Create an equation to find the volume of the pool. You should use the following symbols in your equation:
$Volume\ of\ pool = v$
$Width\ of\ pool = 2x$
$Length\ of\ pool = 3x + 1$
$Height\ of\ pool = 5$

9) James has x pence. Ravi has twenty more pence than James. Sonia has 50 more pence than Ravi. Create an equation showing the total amount of money, in pence, held by the friends. You should use the following symbols in your equation:
$Total\ amount\ of\ money = m$
$Pence\ held\ by\ James = x$
$Pence\ held\ by\ Ravi = (x + 20)$
$Pence\ held\ by\ Sonia = (x + 20 + 50)$

10) Create an equation to describe the angles in the triangle below. You should use the expressions given in the diagram to help you.

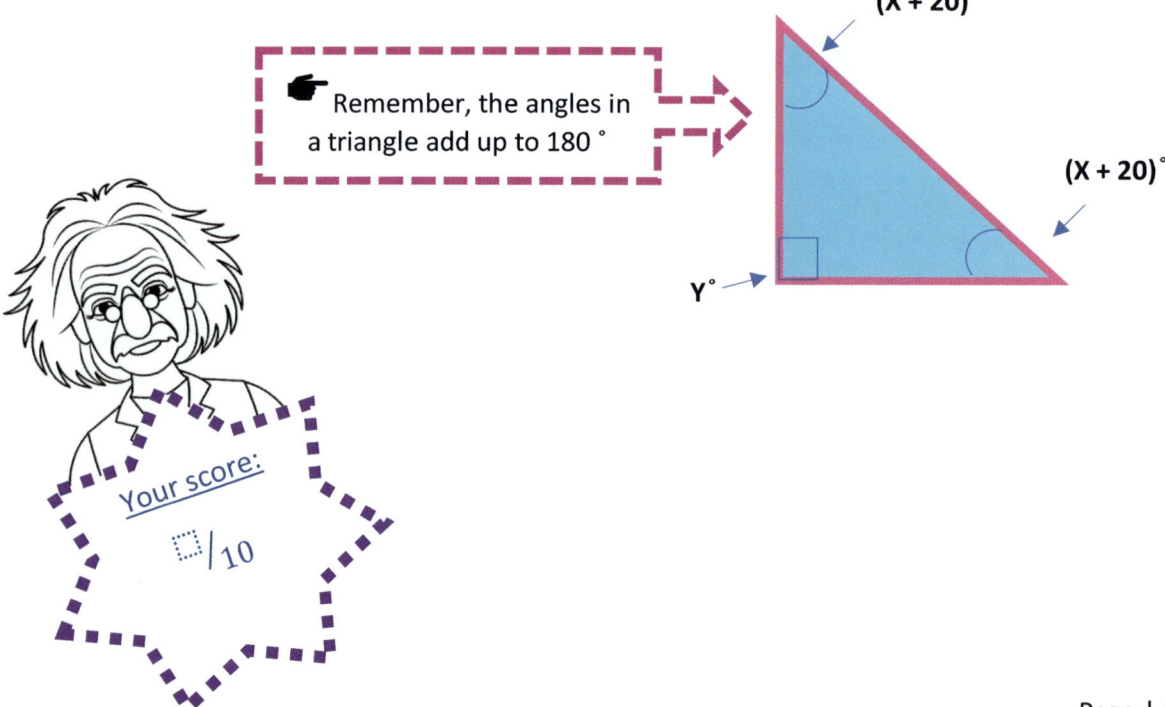

Remember, the angles in a triangle add up to 180°

Your score:
☐/10

Lesson 3: Using simple equations to calculate things.

Now we have an equation let's use it! I go to the supermarket and buy 15 apples and 20 bananas. How can I use my equation from Lesson 2 to calculate the total cost?

Step 1: Write down your equation.

$T = 45A + 30B$

Step 2: Decide what your variables are. Variables are the letters on the right-hand side of your equals sign and they can take any value.

Here my variables are A (number of apples) and B (number of bananas).

Step 3: Write down the values you have for your variables.

$A \text{ (number of apples)} = 15$

$B \text{ (number of bananas)} = 20$

Step 4: Put your numbers into your equation and complete the calculation!

$T = 45A + 30B$

$T = (45 \times 15) + (30 \times 20)$

$T = 675 + 600$

$T = 1275p$

👉 Remember the cost per apples and bananas was in pence so the answer is in pence too!

You can probably tell that this isn't the most sensible way to give our answer, after all when you are visiting the shops the prices are usually displayed in pounds, not pence.

To convert from pounds to pence all we must do is divide the cost in pence by 100.

$1275p \div 100 = £12.75$

Therefore, the total cost, in pounds, is £12.75.

© Sarah Louise Chauhan 2019 – *copying, sharing or unauthorised distribution of this document in part or whole in any public arena including online is strictly prohibited. Action will be taken against any companies, organisations or individuals found to be in breach of these rules.*

Worked example 1.

📄 I am planning a birthday party for my best friend Priya. We plan to give 4 chocolate frogs to each of the adults who come to the party and 3 chocolate frogs to each of the children.

Create an equation which would help me calculate the total number of chocolate frogs I need to buy. You should use the following symbols in your equation:

Total number of frogs = T

Number of adults = A

Number of children = C

If we wrote this as a word equation it would look something like this:

Total number of chocolate frogs = (4 x number of adults) + (3 x number of children)

When we add symbols in it becomes:

T = 4A + 3C

📄 **Use your equation to calculate how many chocolate frogs I need to buy if I expect 11 adults and 32 children to attend the party.**

Step 1: Write down your equation

T = 4A + 3C

Step 2: Decide what your variables are. Remember variables are the letters on the right-hand side of your equals sign and can take any value.

Here my variables are A (number of adults) and B (number of children).

Step 3: Write down the values you have for your variables.

A (number of adults) = 11

C (number of children) = 32

Step 4: Put your numbers into your equation and complete the calculation!

T = 4A + 3C

T = (4 X 11) + (3 X 32)

T = 140

I need 140 chocolate frogs for the party!

Worked example 2.

📄 **Jagdeep picks Tulips and Daffodils from his grandma's garden. He puts the flowers together and splits them into two bunches, one for his grandma and one for his mom.**

Create an equation to calculate how many flowers will be in each bunch. You should use the following symbols for your equation:

$T = Total\ flowers$

$T = Tulips$

$D = Daffodils$

> 🧠 **Important!** When using algebra, we NEVER use the ÷ symbol. Instead writing letters or symbols over a number means divide. For example, $\frac{x}{4}$ means x divided by 4.

If we wrote this as a word equation it would look like this:

$Number\ of\ flowers\ per\ bunch = \frac{(Tulips\ picked + Daffodils\ picked)}{2}$

Next, we need to convert this into an equation.

$T = \frac{(T + D)}{2}$

> 👉 Remember we put the brackets in to show what needs to be done first. We must add the number of Tulips and Daffodils together first, before we divide by two.

📄 **Use your equation to work out how many flowers will be in the bunches if Jagdeep picks 26 Tulips and 48 Daffodils.**

Step 1: Write down your equation

$T = \frac{(T + D)}{2}$

Step 2: Decide what your variables are. Variables are the letters on the right-hand side of your equals sign.

Here my variables are T (number of Tulips) and D (number of daffodils).

Step 3: Write down the values you have for your variables.

$T\ (number\ of\ Tulips) = 26$

$D\ (number\ of\ Daffodils) = 48$

Step 4: Put your numbers into your equation and complete the calculation!

$T = \frac{(T + D)}{2}$

$T = \frac{(26 + 48)}{2}$

$T = \frac{74}{2}$

$T = 37$

Jagdeep will have 37 flowers in each bunch.

Exercise 3.

This exercise will test your knowledge of Book Objective 3. Use the worked answer booklet to check your answers. You will find extra questions for all of the Book Objectives in the end of topic assessment.

1) Using the equation below, find the value of F when x = 12 and Y = 24.
$$F = X + Y$$

2) Using the equation below, find the value of R when J = 34 and T = 3.
$$R = \frac{J - 4}{T}$$

3) Using the equation below, find the value of T when Y = 45.
$$T = \frac{Y}{9} + 12$$

4) Using the equation below, find the value of P when T= 4 and G = 2
$$P = T^2 - G$$

5) Using the equation below, find the value of F when S = 5, H = 3 and K = 4
$$F = (S - H)^2 - K$$

6) Using the equation below, find the value of V when Y = 6, T = 3 and P = 5.
$$V = \left(\frac{Y}{T}\right)^2 + P$$

7) Using the equation below, find the value of Z when T=2 and U=6
$$Z = TU$$

8) Using the equation below, find the value of Z when T = 2 and U =6
$$Z = TU^2$$

9) Using the equation below, find the value of Z when T=2 U = 6
$$Z = (TU)^2$$

10) Using the equation below, find the value of Y when P = 3 and F = 12.
$$Y = \left(P\left(\frac{F}{P}\right)\right)^2$$

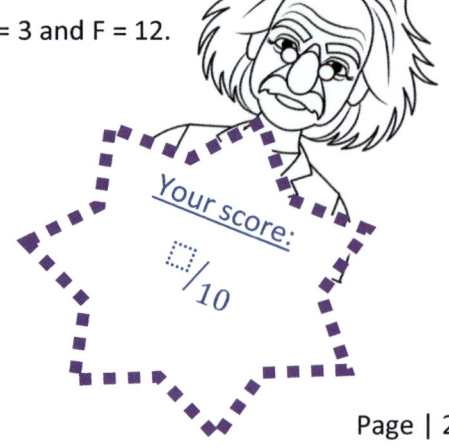

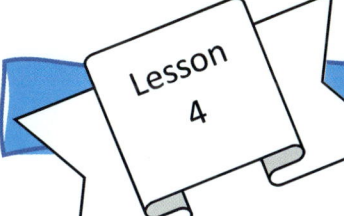

Rearranging equations to change the variable.

When we look at equations the two main parts are the subject and the variables. For example:

$$A = 2B + 5C$$

Here A is the subject – it is the thing that comes before the equals sign and is the thing we are trying to find.

Here B and C are the variables – they are the things which we will put numbers into.

When you are asked to 'rearrange an equation' what you are being asked to do is to change the subject. So instead of A = you might want to find B= or C=. This sounds tricky, but it really isn't once you've got the hang of it.

 Important! There are two key rules when rearranging equations

1) Move everything away from the thing you are trying to make the subject.
2) Whenever a number, letter or symbol goes over to the other side of the equals sign it does the opposite thing to what it was doing before.

Imagine that I have the following equation and want to rearrange it to make A the subject;

$$V = U + AT$$

Step 1: Here V is currently the subject, in order to make A the subject I need to move everything away from it.

When doing this I need to move the things furthest from the A first. In this case U is the furthest thing away from A.

On the RHS (right hand side) of the equals sign it is +U so moving it over to the LHS (left hand side) of the equals sign makes it – U. This gives us:

$$V - U = AT$$

Step 2: Now we must move the T away from the A. On the RHS we have AT which means A x T. As T is being multiplied on the RHS it must become ÷ T on the LHS. This gives us:

$$\frac{V - U}{T} = A$$

Step 3: As the task was to make A the subject it should go on the LHS. We can simply flip the equation to achieve this.

$$A = \frac{V - U}{T}$$

Worked example 1.

 Imagine that we have the following equation and want to rearrange it to make Z the subject:

$Y = Z + 10$

Step 1:

Luckily here there is only one thing which I need to move away from Z to get it on its own. The + 10 needs to go over to the other side of the = sign.

As the opposite of +10 is -10 my formula becomes

$Y - 10 = Z$

Step 2: We can turn this around to make it look more like a regular equation, where the subject is on the LHS.

$Z = Y - 10$

> ☞ Remember when anything goes over the equals sign it becomes the opposite of what it used to be.
>
> *Add and subtract are opposite.*
>
> *Divide and multiply are opposite.*
>
> *Square and square root are opposite.*

Worked example 2.

 The following equation has Y as the subject. Rearrange the equation to make D the subject.

$Y = \dfrac{D - 10}{Z}$

This example is more difficult than the last one as there is lots more going on.

Step 1: We need to remove everything from around the D to get it on its own. When you are doing this, you should always remove the things closest to your desired subject last.

Here the -10 is closest to D, so we remove Z first instead. When it's on the right-hand side it is ÷ Z, when we take it over to the other side of the = we must do the opposite. What is the opposite of divide? Of course, it is multiply. So, our equation becomes:

$YZ = D - 10$

Step 2: We have one thing left to remove from D to get it on its own, this is -10. Again, we will take this to the other side of the equals sign, remembering that as we do so it becomes the opposite of what it was on the RHS. What is the opposite of -10? Well of course it is + 10, so now our equation becomes:

$(YZ) + 10 = D$

> 🧠 **Important!** The YZ is in brackets to show that we must multiply Y and Z this before adding 10.

Step 3: We must now turn this equation around to make it look more like a normal equation with the subject on the LHS. It now becomes:

$D = (YZ) + 10$

Worked example 3.

 The following equation has F as the subject. Rearrange it to make A the subject.

$F = K + 10A^2$

Step 1: We need to remove everything from around A, leaving the closest thing until last. 10 is the closest thing to A, so we must first remove K.

On the right-hand side K is being added to something. Therefore, when we take it over to the other side of the = sign it must become – K. So now we have:

$F - K = 10A$

Step 2: We must now remove the 10 from the A. What does 10A mean? Well remember, numbers are placed together like that when they are being multiplied. Therefore, when we move the 10 to the other side of the equals sign it becomes ÷ 10. Here you need to remember that in algebra we do not use the ÷ symbol, instead it would be written as:

$$\frac{F - K}{10} = A^2$$

Step 3: Now we need to remove the ^{2} from A^2. This is because we want A to be the subject, not A^2.

In order to do this, we need to take the ^{2} over the other side and make it opposite to what it was. What is the opposite of ^{2}? Well the opposite of squaring something is to square root it.

Therefore, we square root the whole of the left-hand side of the equation. Our equation now becomes:

$$\sqrt{\frac{F - K}{10}} = A$$

Step 4: Finally, you must turn this equation around to make the subject, A, appear on the LHS.

$$A = \sqrt{\frac{F - K}{10}}$$

Exercise 4.

This exercise will test your knowledge of Book Objective 4. Use the worked answer booklet to check your answers. You will find extra questions for all of the Book Objectives in the end of topic assessment.

Rearrange the following equations to make K the subject.

1) $T = KY$

2) $T = K + 25$

3) $T = \dfrac{K - 20}{3}$

4) $T = \left(\dfrac{K}{3}\right) - 20$

5) $T = \dfrac{7K + Y}{E}$

6) $T = K^2 + 12$

7) $T = KY + 2$

8) $T = K^2$

9) $T = \sqrt{K}$

10) $T = (KY)^2$

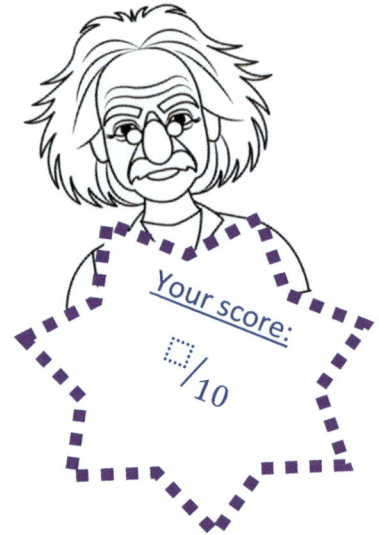

Lesson 5: Rearranging equations to find the solution.

Some equations will only have one variable (symbol or letter). In these equations it is very easy to solve them – this means to find the value of the missing variable.

Let's take a look at an example:

The number of cookies (we will give them the symbol C) needed by Amir for his cookie stall is given by the following equation.

$350 = 5C - 150$

Here we can see there is only one variable, this is C. As there is only one variable mixed in with a group of numbers we can use the equation to find the value of C. This will tell us exactly how many cookies Amir needs for his cookie stall.

In order to do this all we need to do is rearrange the equation to make C the subject, just like we did in Lesson 4.

Step 1: As the – 150 is the furthest away from C we are going to move it away to the LHS first.

This gives us:

$350 + 150 = 5C$

Which is the same as:

$500 = 5C$

👉 Remember when a number, symbol or letter goes to the opposite side of the equals sign it becomes the opposite of what it used to be.

🧠 **Important!** It is key to simplify the equation as you go along. Here it is clear to see that 350 + 150 = 500. Not simplifying as you go through the steps will make the equation more confusing and difficult to deal with at the end.

Step 2: We now need to remove the 5 from the C. As the 5 is multiply by 5 on the RHS when we move it to the LHS it becomes divide by 5. This gives:

$\frac{500}{5} = C$

Again, we must simplify the equation, this gives us:

$100 = C$

Step 3: Finally, we must flip the equation to give C, the subject, on the LHS. This gives us:

$C = 100$

Amir needs 100 cookies for his cookie stall.

© Sarah Louise Chauhan 2019 – *copying, sharing or unauthorised distribution of this document in part or whole in any public arena including online is strictly prohibited. Action will be taken against any companies, organisations or individuals found to be in breach of these rules.*

Worked example 1.

Ly is calculating the amount of profit (£P) she will make from her Veterinary surgery. He accountant, Sidney, has told her that she should use the following equation to find the amount of profit she will make:

$$50,000 = \frac{P}{1.5} - 10,000$$

Using the equation above calculate how much profit Ly can expect to make.

Step 1: To find the profit, P, we need to rearrange the equation so that P is the subject. We start by moving the thing furthest away from P the LHS of the equation. In this case it is the − 10, 000. When we move this over to the LHS our equation becomes:

$$50,000 + 10,000 = \frac{P}{1.5}$$

This simplifies to:

$$60,000 = \frac{P}{1.5}$$

Step 2: We must now remove the 1.5 from below P. As on the RHS it is there as ÷ 1.5 on the LHS it becomes x 1.5. This gives us:

$$60,000 \; x \; 1.5 = P$$

Which simplifies to:

$$90,000 = P$$

Step 3: Finally, we must flip the equation so that P, the subject, is on the LHS. This give us:

$$P = 90,000$$

Ly will make £90,000 in profit from her Vets surgery.

Worked example 2.

📄 The equation below can be used to calculate the number of medals (M) won by the Perry Hall Primary school swimming team in a recent swimming gala.

Use the equation to find M.

$45 + 1.5m = 61 - 0.5m$

Step 1: This equation is a little different to the ones we have looked at previously as the subject, m, appears more than once. That's ok though, all we must do is move all of the m's to the LHS and all of the numbers to the RHS.

We will begin by moving the m's to the LHS. This gives us:

$45 + 1.5m + 0.5m = 61$

Step 2: We must simplify the equation as we go along. Looking at the LHS of the equation we can see that we have 45 + 1.5m + 0.5m. By collecting like terms (in this case the m's) our equation become the following:

$45 + 2m = 61$

Step 3: Now we must move the 45 to the RHS of the equation. This will mean that all of our m's are on one side of the equals and everything else is on the other. This gives us:

$2m = 61 - 45$

Which simplifies to:

$2m = 16$

Step 4: Our equation is almost finished. The only problem is that on the LHS we have 2m. We want to find what m is equal to, not what 2m is equal to. Therefore, we must move the 2 to the RHS of the equation. On the LHS it is x2 so on the RHS it becomes ÷ 2 to give the following:

$m = \frac{16}{2}$

This simplifies to:

$m = 8$

Perry Hall won 8 medals at the swimming gala.

Exercise 5.

This exercise will test your knowledge of Book Objective 5. Use the worked answer booklet to check your answers. You will find extra questions for all of the Book Objectives in the extra questions section and the end of topic test.

1) The following equation gives the number of students going to Paris on a school trip. Solve the equation to find P.

   $600 = 4P + 200$

2) The following equation gives the area of a football pitch (A) in square meters. Solve the equation to find A.

   $80,000 = 30,000 + 5A$

3) The following equation gives the number of downloads (D) sold by a record company. Solve the equation to find D.

   $1,000,000 = \dfrac{D - 5,000,000}{5}$

4) The following equation gives the force of attraction (F) between two particles in Newtons. Solve the equation to find F.
   $0.0004 = 100F$

5) The following equation gives the number of endangered Rhinos (R) found in a Ugandan national park during a recent survey. Solve the equation to find R.

   $500 = 20\sqrt{R}$

6) The following equation gives the number of people who joined Summerfield gym on April 14th 2018 (S). Solve the equation to find S.

   $850 = S^2 - 750$

7) Solve the following to find m:

   $8m - 14 = 3m + 46$

8) Solve the following to find X:

   $3(4X - 5) = 5(2X - 5)$

9) Solve the following to find g:

   $7g - 20 = 2g - 10$

10) Solve the following to find j:

    $20 + \dfrac{1}{2}j = 10 - \dfrac{1}{2}j$

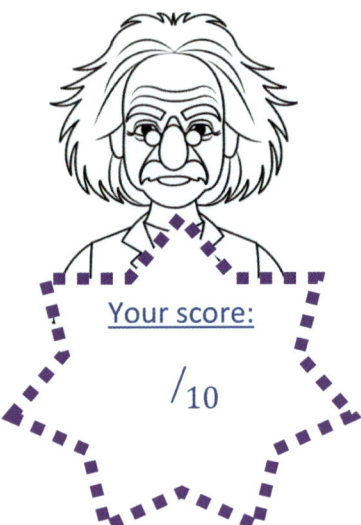

Your score:

/10

Page | 28

© Sarah Louise Chauhan 2019 – copying, sharing or unauthorised distribution of this document in part or whole in any public arena including online is strictly prohibited. Action will be taken against any companies, organisations or individuals found to be in breach of these rules.

Lesson 6: Suggesting values for missing numbers.

Let us think about the following formula:

$A + A + B = 10$

We cannot solve this simply by rearranging as there are two variables, A and B. When given a question like this you will have to suggest what the variables are given limited information.

The only things we know here is that A must be the same both times it appears and when B is added in the total is 10.

Step 1: The first step is to try some values of A. Let's imagine A is 7.

If $A = 7$ then $A + A = 14$. This is clearly too much as the total for the whole equation should be 10.

Next let's try $A = 3$. If $A = 3$ then $A + A = 6$.

Step 2: Based on $A + A = 6$ we must complete the equation by giving a value for B.

Our initial equation was:

$A + A + B = 10$

When $A = 3$

$3 + 3 + B = 10$

Which simplifies to:

$6 + B = 10$

When rearranged gives:

$B = 10 - 6$

$B = 4$

In this case B must equal 4.

Step 3: Finally, we must check our answer by substituting in all of our values together.

Our initial equation was:

$A + A + B = 10$

When $A = 3$ and $B = 4$

$3 + 3 + 4 = 10$

Important! It is important to realise that this is not the only correct combination. For example; if A= 2 then B=6, or if A=1 then B=8. There are plenty of other correct answers. For these types of questions most of the time you will be able to quickly calculate the answer in your head without writing anything down.

When A = 3 B = 4

Worked example 1.

📄 **The following table contains various shapes with different values. Use the row and column totals to determine the value of each of the shapes.**

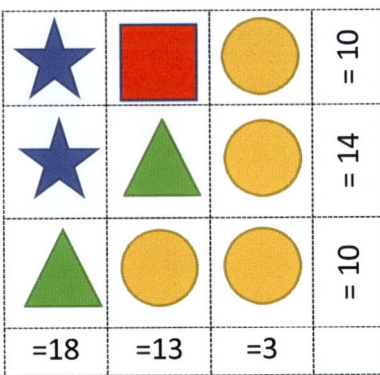

Step 1: First, we must select the easiest column or row to start with. If there is a column or row with all the same shape or symbol this will be it. In this case it is the column with the three yellow circles in it.

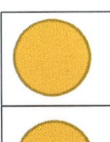
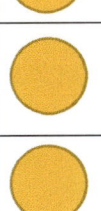

If three yellow circles equal three when added together then it is easy to see that each yellow circle must be equal to one (3 ÷ 3 = 1).

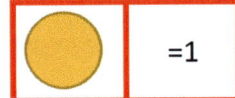

Step 2: Once the first shapes value has been identified the whole task becomes a lot easier. Looking at the table the row we should tackle next is:

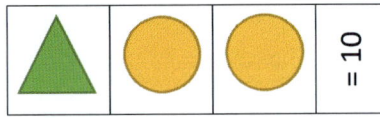

This is because it only has two variables in it (the triangle and the circle) and we already know the value of one of them.

If the circles are worth 1 each then two circles are worth 2. As the whole row added together is equal to 10 this must mean that the triangle is worth 8.

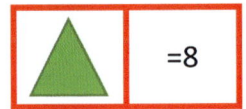

© Sarah Louise Chauhan 2019 – *copying, sharing or unauthorised distribution of this document in part or whole in any public arena including online is strictly prohibited. Action will be taken against any companies, organisations or individuals found to be in breach of these rules.*

Step 3: As we have now found the value of two of our variables it makes sense to tackle the following row next:

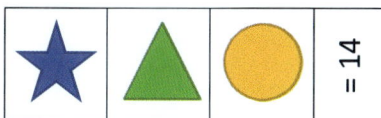

This is because this row only has one unknown variable in it. We must find the value of the star but we already know the value of the triangle and circle. If the triangle is worth 10 and the circle is worth 1 then combined, they have a value of 11. This means that the star must be worth 5.

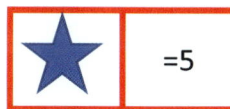

Step 4: We now only have one shape left to find the value of. This is the red square. Looking at one of the rows with the square in we can see that we have the other two shapes:

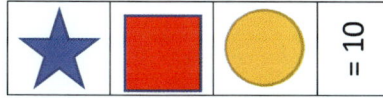

As we know that the circle has a value of 1, the star has a value of 5 and the whole row is worth 10 it is now easy to see that the square has a value of 4.

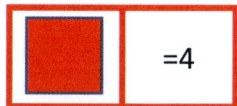

Step 5: Our final step must be to check our answers. The way we do this is to select a column or row which we have not yet used and make sure that our values for the shapes add up to the column or row total.

We will look at the following column:

We know the red square is worth 4, the green triangle is worth 8 and the circle is worth 1. If our numbers are correct these will add up to the column total of 13.

4 + 8 + 1 = 13

As our total is correct, we can be confident that our values are correct.

=13

Page | 31

© Sarah Louise Chauhan 2019 – *copying, sharing or unauthorised distribution of this document in part or whole in any public arena including online is strictly prohibited. Action will be taken against any companies, organisations or individuals found to be in breach of these rules.*

# Exercise 6.

This exercise will test your knowledge of Book Objective 6. Use the worked answer booklet to check your answers. You will find extra questions for all of the Book Objectives in the extra questions section and the end of topic test.

1) A and B are variables in the following equation: $A + A + B = 25$. Suggest values for A and B.

2) C and D are variables in the following equation: $2C + D = 13$. Suggest values for C and D.

3) E, F and G are variables in the following equation: $4E + F - G = 12$. If $G = 20$ suggest values for E and F.

4) H, I and J are variables in the following equation: $\frac{5H + I + J}{2} = 20$.

   If $I = 9$ suggest values for H and J.

5) Look at the following symbol equation. If the δ symbol has a value of 4, what is the value of the μ symbol?
   $$\delta(\mu - \delta) = 24$$

6) Use the following algebra grid to find the value of each of the shapes in it. There is one mark for each correct shape.

♥	⚡	◎	= 19
♥	☾	♥	= 23
♥	☺	◎	= 14
= 27	= 14	= 15	

Your score: ☐/10

Lesson 7: Solving complex word problems by forming

This final lesson represents one of the most difficult style of question you may be asked in your 11+ exam. In the type of question covered here you will be given a short paragraph detailing a problem. From the information given in a problem you will then have to create an equation which you will then solve to answer the question.

Let's imagine that you have been given the following problem:

Last month three boys scored 45 goals between them for their school football team. Ryan scored 3 times as many goals as Tanveer, who scored twice as many goals as Clinton. Calculate the number of goals scored by each of the boys.

Step 1: The first step here would be to decide a symbol or letter for the number of goals scored by each of the boys. It does not matter which letter or symbol you pick so we will use the letter g.

Step 2: We must now create a ratio of goals for the boys.

To create a ratio we will always start with the person who scored the least goals and make their part of the ratio equal to one. In this case Clinton scored the least goals so we will make his part of the ratio equal to 1g. We have created a table to display this information.

Clinton		
1g		

The person who scored the next lowest number of goals was Tanveer who scored twice as many goals as Clinton. By multiplying Clinton's 1g by 2 we get 2g.

Clinton	Tanveer	
1g	2g	

Our highest scorer was Ryan, who scored 3 times as many goals as Tanveer. If we multiply Tanveer's 2g by 3 we get 6g

Clinton	Tanveer	Ryan
1g	2g	6g

Page | 33

© Sarah Louise Chauhan 2019 – *copying, sharing or unauthorised distribution of this document in part or whole in any public arena including online is strictly prohibited. Action will be taken against any companies, organisations or individuals found to be in breach of these rules.*

Step 3: Using our ratio we must now create an overall equation. We can see than Clinton has scored 1g, Tanveer 2g and Ryan 6g.

Putting our ratio into an equation we get the following:

Goals scored by Clinton + Goals scored by Tanveer + Goals scored by Ryan = 45

$1g + 2g + 6g = 45$

Which can simplify to:

$9g = 45$

Step 4: We must now solve the equation to find g.

$9g = 45$

$g = \dfrac{45}{9}$

$g = 5$

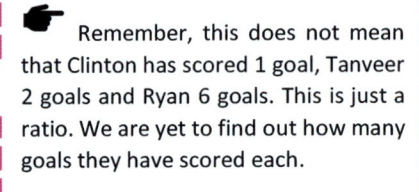

Remember, this does not mean that Clinton has scored 1 goal, Tanveer 2 goals and Ryan 6 goals. This is just a ratio. We are yet to find out how many goals they have scored each.

Step 5: We can now substitute this back into our ratio to find out how many goals each boy scored.

Clinton	Tanveer	Ryan
1g	2g	6g
1 x 5= 5	2 x 5 = 10	6 x 5 = 30
5	10	30

By substituting in g for each of our boys we can see that Clinton scored 5 goals, Tanveer scored 10 goals and Ryan scored 30 goals.

Step 6: Check your answer. An excellent student always checks their answers. In the original part of the question we were told that in total the boys scored 45 goals. We must now check that our number of goals for the boys totals 45.

$5 + 10 + 30 = 45$

The goals scored add up to the total we expect. We can accept our answers as correct.

© Sarah Louise Chauhan 2019 – *copying, sharing or unauthorised distribution of this document in part or whole in any public arena including online is strictly prohibited. Action will be taken against any companies, organisations or individuals found to be in breach of these rules.*

Worked example 1.

📄 A hospital in London is collecting donations of teddy bears for sick children from two areas. In total the hospital collects 2794 teddy bears. People in Lewisham collect 232 more teddy bears than people in Croydon. Calculate the number of teddy bears donated by each area.

Step 1: The first step is to decide on a symbol or letter for the teddys, we will choose the letter t.

Step 2: We must now create an expression for the number of teddy bears collected by each area. This question is slightly different from the last as people in Lewisham collect 232 more teddy bears than people in Croydon, not 232 times more teddy bears than people in Lewisham.

> 🧠 **Important!** If people in Lewisham had collected 232 times more teddy bears than people in Croydon our expressions would be Croydon t teddy bears and Lewisham $232t$ teddy bears.

Therefore, people in Croydon collect t teddy bears, and people in Lewisham collect $t + 232$ teddy bears.

Step 3: The next step is to take our individual expressions and turn them into one equation. The total number of teddy bears collected was 2794 therefore our complete equation is:

Bears collected by Croydon + Bears collected by Lewisham = 2794

$t + (t + 232) = 2794$

Which simplifies to:

$2t + 232 = 2794$

Step 4: We must now solve this equation to find t.

$2t + 232 = 2794$

$2t = 2794 - 232$

$2t = 2562$

$t = \dfrac{2562}{2}$

$t = 1281$

Step 5: We must substitute our value for t back into our expressions for the two areas to find out how many teddy bears they each donated.

Croydon	Lewisham
t	$t + 232$
1281	1513

Step 6: Finally, we must check that our answers are correct by making sure that they add up to the expected total of 2794.

No. of teddys collected in Croydon + No. of teddys collected in Lewisham = 2794

$1281 + 1513 = 2794$

Our total is as expected so we can accept our answer.

© Sarah Louise Chauhan 2019 – *copying, sharing or unauthorised distribution of this document in part or whole in any public arena including online is strictly prohibited. Action will be taken against any companies, organisations or individuals found to be in breach of these rules.*

Exercise 7.

This exercise will test your knowledge of Book Objective 7. Use the worked answer booklet to check your answers. You will find extra questions for all of the Book Objectives in the extra questions section and the end of topic test.

1) In April three workers at an electronics store were having a competition to sell tablets. Yasmin sold four times as many tablets as Greg, who sold 3 times as many tablets as Fasil. The group sold 64 tablets in total. Calculate how many tablets each one of them sold.
2) The total age of me, my mom and my grandad is 143. My mom is three times as old as me, and my grandad is three times as old as her. How old am I?
3) In a recent cards game three friends had a total of 525 points. Charlie had six times as many points as Francesca, who had twice as many points as Ishty. Calculate how many points each of the friends had.
4) During the summer holidays two friends, Carl and Nazir, open a shop selling surf boards. Nazir sells 2 ½ times the number of surf boards that Carl does. They sell 42 surf boards in total. How many boards does each friend sell?
5) Cheese is a popular French export. Last year France exported 5 times as much Gruyere cheese as Camembert. It exported 4 times as much Camembert as Brie, and 2 times as much Brie as Pavin. In total France exported 306 tonnes of cheese. Calculate how many tonnes of each cheese it exported last year.
6) The Bank of England is minting some new coins. It creates 12 times as many 50p coins as it does £1 coins and creates 7 times as many £1 coins as it does 20p coins. In total the Bank of England creates 230,000 new coins. How many of each coin does it create? What is the value, in pounds, of all of the coins created?
7) Dawn is a motivational speaker. During her last seminar there were twice as many people over 35 than there were people under 35. Her seminar attracted 990 attendees. How many people at the seminar were over 35?
8) Whilst Skiing in France Gurpreet discovered that in 2009 there was 5 times as much snow on the mountains as in 2015. In 2015 there was twice as much snowfall on the mountains as in 2018. Over the three years mentioned there was 702 tonnes of snowfall on the mountains. Calculate how much snowfall was present in each individual year.
9) Terry is building a pagoda for his garden. He needs four pieces of wood to complete the last part of the project. Plank A is three times the length of plank B. Plank B is twice as long as plank C. Plank D is the same length as plank C. In total these planks of wood have a length of 60 meters. Calculate the length of each plank of wood.
10) Chester is opening a new café in his local city. His budget for furniture is twice his budget for cutlery. His budget for cutlery is 50% more than his budget for leaflets. His total budget is £4,900. Calculate how much money he has budgeted to spend on each item.

Your score: ☐/10

Page | 36

© Sarah Louise Chauhan 2019 – *copying, sharing or unauthorised distribution of this document in part or whole in any public arena including online is strictly prohibited. Action will be taken against any companies, organisations or individuals found to be in breach of these rules.*

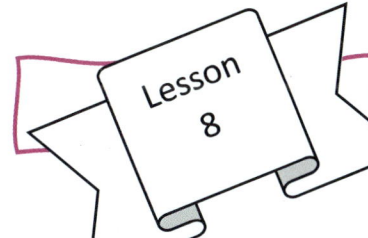

Lesson 8: End of topic assessment (50 mins approx.)

1) Tiffany is opening a makeup stall in her local market. She hires the stall for £S and buys 81 contour kits to sell on the stall. The contour kits come in boxes of 9 and cost £C per box. How much money has Tiffany spent setting up her stall? Create an equation to express how much money Tiffany has spent setting up her stall. You should use the following symbols in your equation: **(1 mark)**
$M = Money\ spent\ by\ Tiffany\ in\ total$
$S = Cost\ of\ stall\ hire$
$C = Cost\ of\ contour\ kits\ per\ box$

2) Sohal is looking to buy a house with her sister. They have a deposit of £D and must also pay a fee to their estate agent of £E. Sohal is going to pay 60% of the cost, whereas her sister will pay 40%. Create an equation to express how much money Sohal will pay. You should use the following symbols in your equation: **(1 mark)**
$T = Total\ money\ spent\ by\ Sohal$
$D = Deposit$
$E = Estate\ agent\ fees$

3) Hemel is planting seeds in his greenhouse. He has Y sunflower seeds, S Sweet pea seeds and P Primrose seeds. In his first flower border he plants 75% of the sunflower seeds, 45% of the Sweet pea seeds and 20% of the Primrose seeds. Create an equation to express how many seeds are left for the rest of the garden. You should use the following symbols in your equation: **(1 mark)**
$L = Seeds\ left$
$Y = Sunflower\ seeds$
$S = Sweet\ pea\ seeds$
$P = Primrose\ seeds$

4) Frankie is opening a shoe stall in his local market. He sells 67 pairs of boots and makes £B profit on each pair. He also sells 90 handbags and makes £H profit on each one. From this profit he buys some more stock which costs £S. Create an equation to express how much money Frankie has at the end. You should use the following symbols in your equation: **(1 mark)**
$P = Profit\ left$
$B = Profit\ on\ each\ pair\ of\ boots$
$H = Profit\ on\ each\ handbag$
$S = Cost\ of\ new\ stock$

5) Satya is putting new grass seed down on her garden. Her garden is an unusual triangle shape as shown below with expressions for the length of the width and height. You should use the following symbols in your equation: **(1 mark)**

$A = Area$
$4Y + 8 = Width$
$Y = Height$

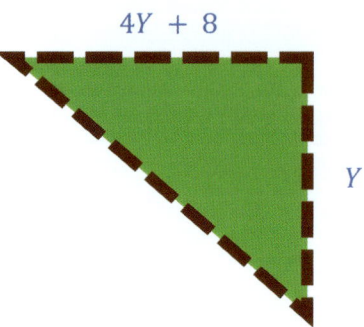

6) Dr Vissa is building a fence for her garden. The dimensions of her garden are shown below. Using these dimensions create an expression for the perimeter of her garden. You should use the following symbols in your equation: **(1 mark)**

$P = Perimeter$
$5x + 2y = Length$
$x - y = Width$

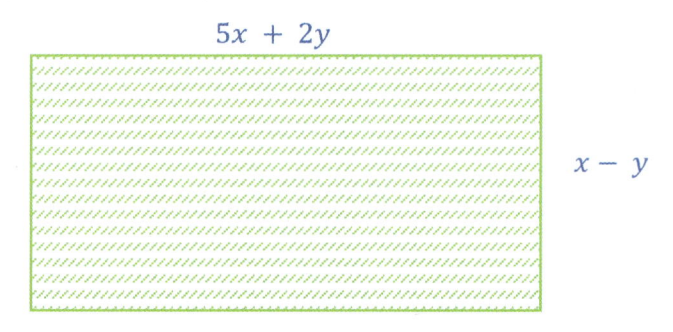

7) If $y = 60$ and $x = 20$ give the value of z in the following equation: **(1 mark)**

$$z = \frac{x(y - x)}{2}$$

8) If $v = 5$ and $c = 12$ give the value of j in the following equation: **(1 mark)**
$j = (v + c)(v - c)$

9) If $b = 2$ and $n = 6$ give the value of i in the following equation: **(1 mark)**

$$i = \frac{b(bn)}{n}$$

10) If $e = 2$ and $r = 9$ give the value of v in the following equation: **(1 mark)**
$(2r + 4e) = v(r + 2e)$

11) If $t = 9$ and $r = 16$ give the value of d in the following equation: **(1 mark)**

$$d = \sqrt{t + r}$$

12) If $a = 4, b = 6$ and $c = 7$ give the value of d in the following equation: **(1 mark)**

$$d = 4a^2 + 2b - c$$

13) Rearrange the following equations to make v the subject: **(1 mark for each correct answer)**
a) $vf - g = h$

b) $\dfrac{g}{v} - h = kl$

c) $\sqrt{yv} = Q$

d) $2h^2 + v = hy$

e) $(h + v)^2 = z$

f) $g\sqrt{\dfrac{v}{h}} = j$

14) Solve the following equations to find the value of i: **(1 mark for each correct answer)**

a) $3i + 4 = i + 13$

b) $2i + 5 = 10$
c) $3 + 6i = 6$
d) $2i + 11 = 17$

e) $7 + 5i = 8i + 1$

f) $4i - 3 = 2i + 27$

g) $\dfrac{10 + 2i}{4} = 7$

h) $3(2i + 4) = i - 13$

i) $i = \dfrac{9i - 15}{12}$

j) $3(2i - 1) + 2(i + 4) = 29$

15) Solve the following to find h: **(1 mark)**

$$\frac{2}{5}h + 30 = 50 - \frac{3}{5}h$$

16) Solve the following to find v: **(1 mark)**

$$5(4v + 20) = -5v - 25$$

17) Solve the following to find q: **(1 mark)**

$$\frac{2}{5}q + 55 = 45 - \frac{3}{5}q$$

18) Solve the following to find n: **(1 mark)**

$$3(n + 2) = 6(n - 2)$$

19) Use the following shape equations to find the value of the shapes given in it. There is one mark for each correct shape. **(1 mark for each correct shape value)**

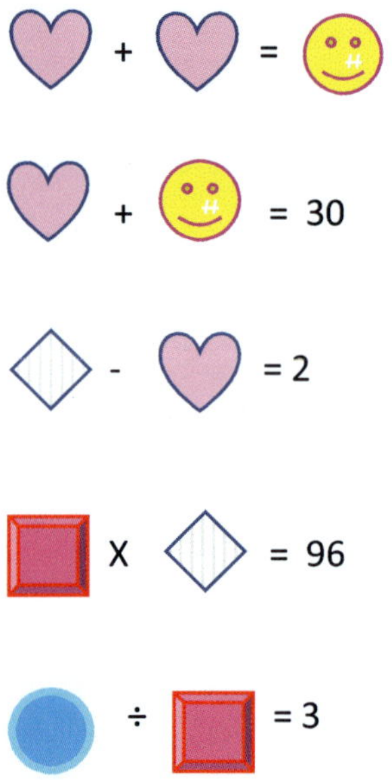

♥ + ♥ = ☺

♥ + ☺ = 30

◇ - ♥ = 2

■ × ◇ = 96

● ÷ ■ = 3

20) Look at the following symbol equation. If the ¥ symbol has a value of 7, what is the value of the α symbol? **(1 mark)**

$$\frac{(\alpha - ¥)}{¥} = 2$$

21) The triangle below has three angles as marked A, B and C. The expressions for each of the individual angles
are as follows:
$(x + 60)° = A$
$(x + 20)° = B$
$2x° = C$

Create an equation to describe all the relationship between all of the angles in the triangle. Use this equation to find the value of x and therefore the value of the angles A, B and C. (Remember the angles in a triangle always add up to 180°). **(2 mark)**

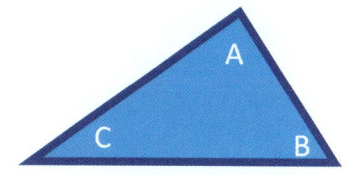

22) The diagram below shows a trapezium. Below you will also find expressions for angles A and B. Using this information and the diagram create an equation to describe the relationship between all of the angles in the trapezium. Then using your equation calculate the value of each of the angles. (Remember the angles in a quadrilateral add up to 360 °). **(2 marks)**

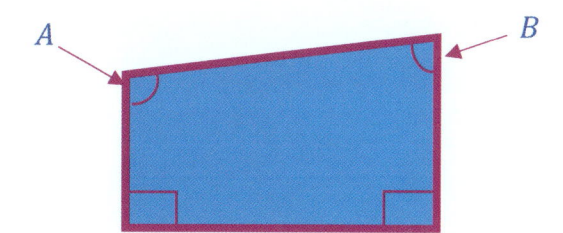

$(x - 20)° = A$

$(x + 20)° = B$

23) Dinesh and Tamzin are looking to buy a house together. Tamzin has been saving for longer and has 4 times as much money saved as Dinesh. In total they have a deposit of £20,000. Create an expression to describe their deposit and use this expression to calculate how much each of them contributes to the deposit. **(2 marks)**

24) Joginder, Susan and Mary are baking cakes. Joginder bakes 3 times as many cakes as Mary. Mary bakes 2 ½ times as many cakes as Susan. In total the friends bake 220 cakes. Create an expression to describe how many cakes are baked by the friends and use this expression to calculate how many each of the friends bake. **(2 marks)**

© Sarah Louise Chauhan 2019 – *copying, sharing or unauthorised distribution of this document in part or whole in any public arena including online is strictly prohibited. Action will be taken against any companies, organisations or individuals found to be in breach of these rules.*

Well done! You have successfully completed Algebra Booster and should now have an excellent understanding of algebra. The score that you have achieved on this end of topic test and in the exercises at the end of each lesson is a great indication of how well you have understood the Book Objectives listed at the beginning of the book.

Remember – the key to success in your 11+, SATS and beyond into life is to learn from your mistakes. If you have got any questions wrong in the end of topic test or in the book exercises you should go back and look at them again. Read again the section of the book which covers that question and attempt it again. This is what separates excellent students from average ones.

Your score: ☐/46

© Sarah Louise Chauhan 2019 – *copying, sharing or unauthorised distribution of this document in part or whole in any public arena including online is strictly prohibited. Action will be taken against any companies, organisations or individuals found to be in breach of these rules.*

Answers – Exercise 1

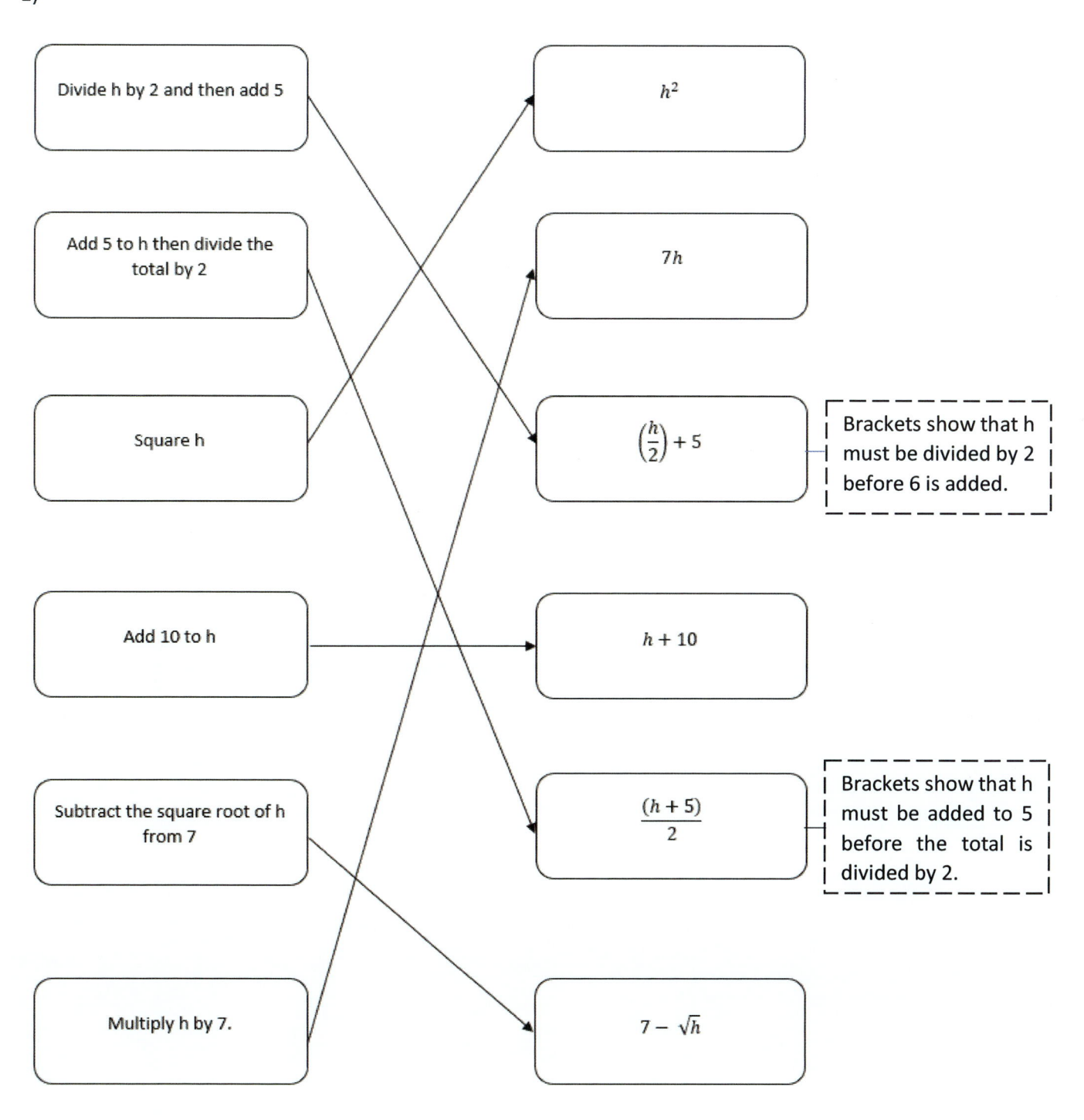

1)

Divide h by 2 and then add 5	h^2
Add 5 to h then divide the total by 2	$7h$
Square h	$\left(\dfrac{h}{2}\right) + 5$ — Brackets show that h must be divided by 2 before 6 is added.
Add 10 to h	$h + 10$
Subtract the square root of h from 7	$\dfrac{(h+5)}{2}$ — Brackets show that h must be added to 5 before the total is divided by 2.
Multiply h by 7.	$7 - \sqrt{h}$

Matches:
- Divide h by 2 and then add 5 → $\left(\dfrac{h}{2}\right) + 5$
- Add 5 to h then divide the total by 2 → $\dfrac{(h+5)}{2}$
- Square h → h^2
- Add 10 to h → $h + 10$
- Subtract the square root of h from 7 → $7 - \sqrt{h}$
- Multiply h by 7 → $7h$

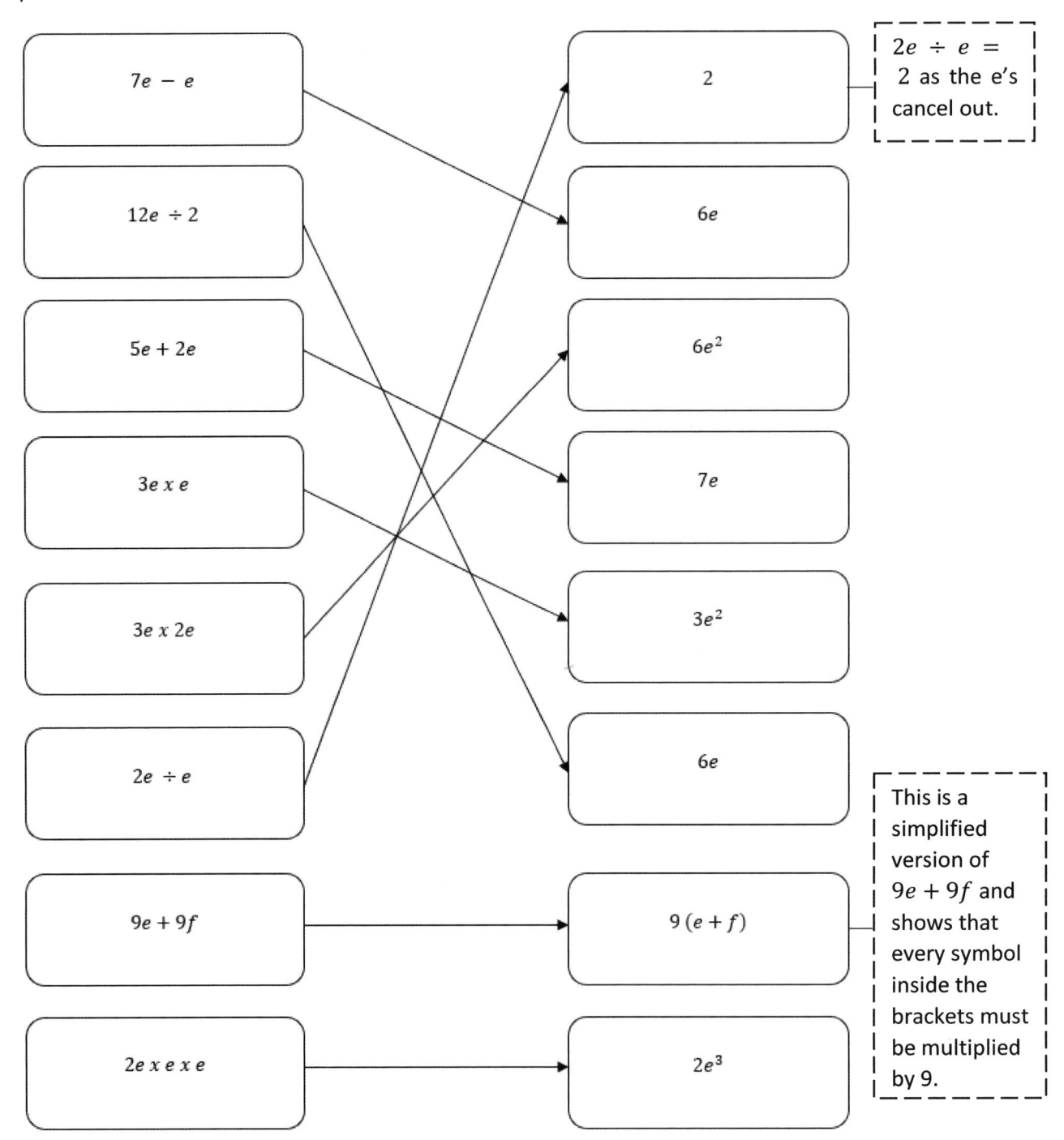

2)

$7e - e$	2
$12e \div 2$	$6e$
$5e + 2e$	$6e^2$
$3e \times e$	$7e$
$3e \times 2e$	$3e^2$
$2e \div e$	$6e$
$9e + 9f$	$9(e + f)$
$2e \times e \times e$	$2e^3$

Matches shown:
- $7e - e \rightarrow 6e$
- $2e \div e \rightarrow 2$ — $2e \div e = 2$ as the e's cancel out.
- $12e \div 2 \rightarrow 6e$
- $5e + 2e \rightarrow 7e$
- $3e \times e \rightarrow 3e^2$
- $3e \times 2e \rightarrow 6e^2$
- $9e + 9f \rightarrow 9(e+f)$ — This is a simplified version of $9e + 9f$ and shows that every symbol inside the brackets must be multiplied by 9.
- $2e \times e \times e \rightarrow 2e^3$

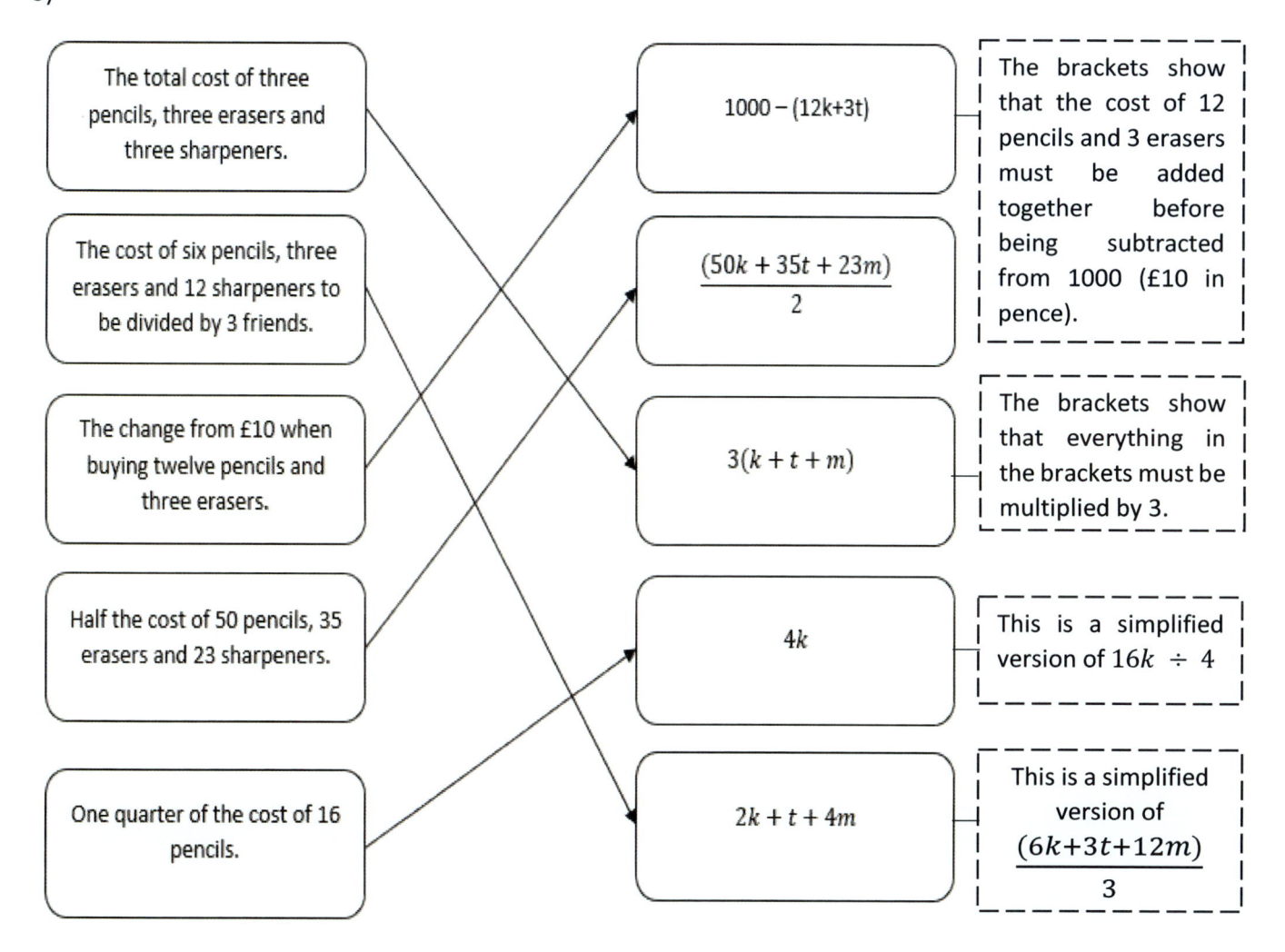

3)

Left box	Right expression	Explanation
The total cost of three pencils, three erasers and three sharpeners.	$1000 - (12k+3t)$	The brackets show that the cost of 12 pencils and 3 erasers must be added together before being subtracted from 1000 (£10 in pence).
The cost of six pencils, three erasers and 12 sharpeners to be divided by 3 friends.	$\dfrac{(50k + 35t + 23m)}{2}$	
The change from £10 when buying twelve pencils and three erasers.	$3(k + t + m)$	The brackets show that everything in the brackets must be multiplied by 3.
Half the cost of 50 pencils, 35 erasers and 23 sharpeners.	$4k$	This is a simplified version of $16k \div 4$
One quarter of the cost of 16 pencils.	$2k + t + 4m$	This is a simplified version of $\dfrac{(6k+3t+12m)}{3}$

Matches:
- The total cost of three pencils, three erasers and three sharpeners → $3(k + t + m)$
- The cost of six pencils, three erasers and 12 sharpeners to be divided by 3 friends → $2k + t + 4m$
- The change from £10 when buying twelve pencils and three erasers → $1000 - (12k+3t)$
- Half the cost of 50 pencils, 35 erasers and 23 sharpeners → $\dfrac{(50k + 35t + 23m)}{2}$
- One quarter of the cost of 16 pencils → $4k$

Answers – Exercise 2

1) $Total\ items = crisps + chocolate + apples$
   $T = R + Y + A$

2) $Rabbits\ left\ at\ the\ end = Rabbits\ for\ sale\ at\ the\ beginning - 3$
   $L = S - 3$

3) $Number\ of\ books\ at\ the\ end = \left(\frac{Number\ of\ books\ at\ the\ beginning}{2}\right) + 20$
   $E = \left(\frac{B}{2}\right) + 20$

Notes: The brackets must be present around B ÷ 2 to show that this part of the calculation must be done before adding 20.

4) $Total\ number\ of\ students = (7\ x\ Number\ of\ students\ in\ each\ minibus) + (4\ x\ number\ of\ students\ in\ each\ car)$
   $S = (7M) + (4C)$

5) $Tadpoles\ at\ the\ end = \frac{(Tadpoles\ at\ the\ start - 5)}{2}$
   $E = \frac{(S - 5)}{2}$

Notes: The brackets must be present around S-5 to show that 5 tadpoles got eaten before the remaining number was halved.

6) $Perimeter = Length\ of\ side\ 1 + Length\ of\ side\ 2 + Length\ of\ side\ 3 + Length\ of\ side\ 4$
   $P = 5D + 4T + 5D + 4T$
   $P = 10D + 8T$

Notes: Here we can collect like terms to simplify the expression. For example; 4T + 4T = 8T. Be careful as terms must be exactly the same. For example; 4T + 4T² cannot be simplified as T and T² are NOT like terms.

7) $Area = Length\ x\ Width$
   $A = 2R\ x\ R$
   $A = 2R^2$

8) Volume = Area of front face x Length

   Volume = Height x Width x Length

   $V = 5 \times 2x \times (3x + 1)$

   $V = 10x(3x + 1)$

   $V = 30x^2 + 10x$

   Notes: To make this problem easier to deal with the best thing to do is to break it into stages where the 5 is multiplied by 2x first, this of course gives us 10x. We then multiply everything in the brackets by 10x to give the correct final answer.

9) Total amount of money = Pence held by James + Pence held by Ravi + Pence held by Sonia.

   $m = x + (x + 20) + (x + 20 + 50)$

   $m = 3x + 90$

10) Sum of all angles in the triangle = 180°

   $90 + (x + 20) + (x + 20) = 180°$

   90 + 2x + 40 = 180

   130 + 2x = 180

   Notes: We could then go on to solve this equation and calculate what x is however for this exercise we are just interested in forming an equation.

Answers – Exercise 3

1) $F = 12 + 24$
   $F = 36$

2) $R = \frac{34 - 4}{3}$
   $R = 10$

3) $T = \frac{45}{9} + 12$
   $T = 5 + 12$
   $T = 17$

4) $P = 4^2 - 2$
   $P = 16 - 2$
   $P = 14$

5) $F = (5 - 3)^2 - 4$
   $F = (2)^2 - 4$
   $F = 4 - 4$
   $F = 0$

6) $V = \left(\frac{6}{3}\right)^2 + 5$
   $V = (2)^2 + 5$
   $V = 4 + 5$
   $V = 9$

7) Z = 2 x 6
   Z = 12

8) Z = 2 x 6^2
   Z = 2 x 36
   Z = 72

9) Z = (2 X 6)^2
   Z = 12^2
   Z = 144

10) $Y = \left(3\left(\frac{12}{3}\right)\right)^2$
    $Y = (3 \; X \; 4)^2$
    $Y = 12^2$
    $Y = 144$

Answers – Exercise 4

1) $600 = 4P + 200$
   $600 - 200 = 4P$
   $400 = 4P$
   $\dfrac{400}{4} = P$
   $100 = P$
   $P = 100$

2) $80{,}000 = 30{,}000 + 5A$
   $80{,}000 - 30{,}000 = 5A$
   $50{,}000 = 5A$
   $\dfrac{50{,}000}{5} = A$
   $10{,}000 = A$
   $A = 10{,}000$

3) $1{,}000{,}000 = \dfrac{D - 5{,}000{,}000}{5}$
   $1{,}000{,}000 \; x \; 5 = D - 5{,}000{,}000$
   $5{,}000{,}000 = D - 5{,}000{,}000$
   $5{,}000{,}000 + 5{,}000{,}000 = D$
   $10{,}000{,}000 = D$
   $D = 10{,}000{,}000$

4) $0.0004 = 100F$
   $(0.0004)/100 = F$
   $0.000004 = F$
   $F = 0.000004$

5) $500 = 20\sqrt{R}$
   $\dfrac{500}{20} = \sqrt{R}$
   $25 = \sqrt{R}$
   $25^2 = R$
   $R = 625$

6) $850 = S^2 - 750$
   $850 + 750 = S^2$
   $1600 = S^2$
   $\sqrt{1600} = S$
   $40 = S$
   $S = 40$

Page | 49

© Sarah Louise Chauhan 2019 – *copying, sharing or unauthorised distribution of this document in part or whole in any public arena including online is strictly prohibited. Action will be taken against any companies, organisations or individuals found to be in breach of these rules.*

7) $8m - 14 = 3m + 46$
$8m - 3m = 46 + 14$
$5m = 60$
$m = \dfrac{60}{5}$
$m = 12$

8) $3(4X - 5) = 5(2X - 5)$
$12x - 15 = 10x - 25$
$12x - 10x = -25 + 15$
$2x = -10$
$x = \dfrac{-10}{2}$
$x = -5$

Notes: In this example the two sides of the equation must be multiplied out before it can be simplified.

9) $7g - 20 = 2g - 10$
$7g - 2g = -10 + 20$
$5g = 10$
$g = \dfrac{10}{5}$
$g = 2$

10) $20 + \dfrac{1}{2}j = 10 - \dfrac{1}{2}j$
$20 + \dfrac{1}{2}j + \dfrac{1}{2}j = 10$
$j = 10 - 20$
$j = -10$

Answers – Exercise 5

1) $T = KY$

$\frac{T}{Y} = K$

$K = \frac{T}{Y}$

2) $T = K + 25$

$T - 25 = K$

$K = T - 25$

3) $T = \frac{K - 20}{3}$

$3T = K - 20$

$3T + 20 = K$

$K = 3T + 20$

4) $T = \left(\frac{K}{3}\right) - 20$

$T + 20 = \left(\frac{K}{3}\right)$

$3(T + 20) = K$

$3T + 60 = K$

$K = 3T + 60$

Notes: Here everything on the LHS must be multiplied by 3. Brackets are placed around T+20 to show this. Once the multiplication has taken place then the equation can be simplified.

5) $T = \frac{7K + Y}{E}$

$TE = 7K + Y$

$TE - Y = 7K$

$\frac{TE - Y}{7} = K$

$K = \frac{TE - Y}{7}$

6) $T = K^2 + 12$

   $T - 12 = K^2$

   $\sqrt{T - 12} = K$
   $K = \sqrt{T - 12}$

7) $T = KY + 2$

   $T - 2 = KY$

   $\dfrac{T - 2}{Y} = K$

   $K = \dfrac{T - 2}{Y}$

8) $T = K^2$
   $\sqrt{T} = K$
   $K = \sqrt{T}$

9) $T = \sqrt{K}$

   $T^2 = K$

   $K = T^2$

10) $T = (KY)^2$

    $\sqrt{T} = (KY)$

    $\sqrt{T}\ KY$

    $\dfrac{\sqrt{T}}{Y} = K$

    $K = \dfrac{\sqrt{T}}{Y}$

Answers – Exercise 6

1) $A + A + B = 25$

    $2A + B = 25$

    Here all we know is that the two A's must be the same and B can be different. There are many variations here which are correct some examples are below:

    $A = 10 \; B = 5$

    $A = 5 \; B = 15$

    $A = 2 \; B = 21$

    If your suggestions for A and B give the correct total of 25 then your answer is correct.

2) Again here any suggestions which give the correct total are correct answers, some examples are as follows:

    $C = 5 \; D = 3$

    $C = 4 \; D = 5$

    $C = 3 \; D = 7$

    $C = 2 \; D = 9$

    $C = 1 \; D = 11$

3) Here we know what G is so our first step should be to substitute it into the equation.

    $4E + F - 20 = 12$

    We can now rearrange this to get all the numbers on the RHS and all of our variables on the LHS.

    $4E + F = 12 + 20$

    $4E + F = 32$

    We can now go on to suggest values for E and F. Again, providing that your suggestions for E and F give the correct answer of 32 when put into the equation they are correct. Here are some examples of correct answers.

    $E = 0 \; F = 32$

    $E = 1 \; F = 28$

    $E = 2 \; F = 24$

    $E = 3 \; F = 20$

    $E = 4 \; F = 16$

© Sarah Louise Chauhan 2019 – *copying, sharing or unauthorised distribution of this document in part or whole in any public arena including online is strictly prohibited. Action will be taken against any companies, organisations or individuals found to be in breach of these rules.*

$E = 5 \; F = 12$

$E = 6 \; F = 8$

$E = 7 \; F = 4$

$E = 8 \; F = 0$

4) Here we have a value of I so we must first substitute this into our equation.

$$\frac{5H + 9 + J}{2} = 20$$

We must now rearrange the equation to get all of the numbers possible on the RHS.

$$\frac{5H + 9 + J}{2} = 20$$

$5H + 9 + J = 20 \; X \; 2$

$5H + 9 + J = 40$

$5H + J = 40 - 9$

$5H + J = 31$

We can now go on to suggest values for H and J. Again, providing that your suggestions for H and J give the correct answer of 31 when put into the equation they are correct. Here are some examples of correct answers.

$H = 6 \; J = 1$

$H = 5 \; J = 6$

$H = 4 \; J = 11$

$H = 3 \; J = 16$

$H = 2 \; J = 21$

$H = 1 \; J = 26$

$H = 0 \; J = 31$

5) Here we have a value for δ so we must first substitute this into our equation.

$4(\mu - 4) = 24$

We can now multiply out our equation and simplify it.

$4\mu - 16 = 24$

$4\mu = 24 + 16$

$4\mu = 40$

$$\mu = \frac{40}{4}$$

$$\mu = 10$$

6) Our first step here is to look for a row or column where there is only one symbol.

As 3 x ♥ = 27

Then ♥ = 9

= 27

Now we should look at a row or column where the ♥ appears along with one other symbol.

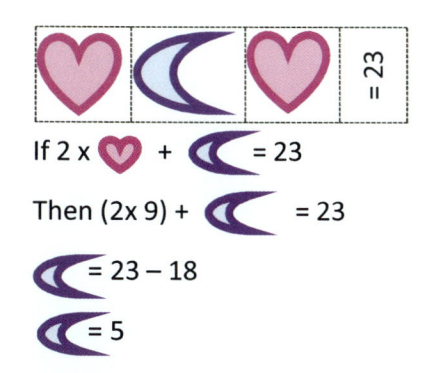

= 23

If 2 x ♥ + ☾ = 23

Then (2x 9) + ☾ = 23

☾ = 23 – 18

☾ = 5

Now we should look at a row or column with either the ♥ or ☾ in it along with something else.

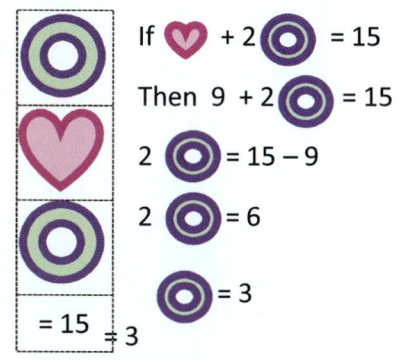

If ♥ + 2◉ = 15

Then 9 + 2◉ = 15

2◉ = 15 – 9

2◉ = 6

◉ = 3

= 15

Now we can look at either of the remaining rows or columns to calculate the value of the remaining missing symbols.

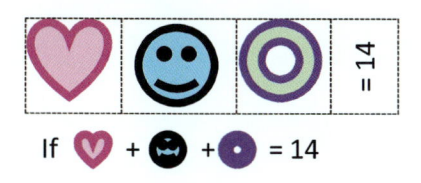

= 14

If ♥ + ☺ + ◉ = 14

Then: 9 + 😠 + 3 = 14

😠 = 14 − 12

😠 = 2

Finally, we can look at the last remaining column:

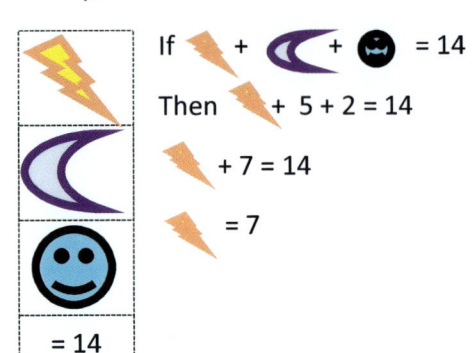

If ⚡ + ☾ + 😠 = 14

Then ⚡ + 5 + 2 = 14

⚡ + 7 = 14

⚡ = 7

Answers – Exercise 7

1)

Fasil	Greg	Yasmin
$1t$	$3t$	$12t$

$1t + 3t + 12t = 64$

$16t = 64$

$t = \dfrac{64}{16}$

$t = 4$

Fasil $= 1t = 1 \times 4 =$ **4 tablets**

Greg $= 3t = 3 \times 4 =$ **12 tablets**

Yasmin $= 12 \times 4 =$ **48 tablets**

2)

me	mom	grandad
a	$3a$	$9a$

$a + 3a + 9a = 143$

$13a = 143$

$a = \dfrac{143}{13}$

$a = 11$

I am 11.

3)

Ishty	Francesca	Charlie
p	$2p$	$12p$

$p + 2p + 12p = 525$

$15p = 525$

$p = \dfrac{525}{15}$

$p = 35$

Ishty = $1 \times p = 1 \times 35$ = **35 points.**

Francesca = $2 \times p = 2 \times 35$ = **70 points.**

Charlie = $12 \times p = 12 \times 35$ = **420 points.**

4)

Carl	Nazir
$1s$	$2 ½ s$

$1s + 2 ½ s = 42$

$3 ½ s = 42$

$s = \dfrac{42}{3.5}$

$s = 12$

Carl = $1 \times s = 1 \times 12$ = **12 surfboards.**

Nazir = $2 ½ \times s = 2 ½ \times 12$ = **30 surfboards.**

5)

Pavin	Brie	Camembert	Gruyere
c	$2c$	$8c$	$40c$

$c + 2c + 8c + 40c = 306$

$51c = 306$

$c = \dfrac{306}{51}$

$c = 6$

Pavin = $1 \, x \, c = 1 \, x \, 6$ = **6 tones.**

Brie = $2 \, x \, c = 2 \, x \, 6$ = **12 tones.**

Camembert = $8 \, x \, c = 8 \, x \, 6$ = **48 tones.**

Gruyere = $40 \, x \, c = 40 \, x \, 6$ = **240 tones.**

6)

20p	50p	£1
c	$84c$	$7c$

$c + 7c + 84c = 230{,}000$

$92c = 230{,}000$

$c = \dfrac{230{,}000}{92}$

$c = 2{,}500$

20p = $1 \, x \, c = 1 \, x \, 2{,}500$ = **2,500 coins minted.**

50p = $84 \, x \, c = 84 \, x \, 2{,}500$ = **210,000 coins minted.**

£1 = $7 \, x \, c = 7 \, x \, 2{,}500$ = **17,500 coins minted.**

The value of these coins is as follows:

2,500 x £0.2 = **£500.**

210,000 x £0.5 = **£ 105,000**

17,500 x £1 = **£17,500**

In total the value of all of the coins created is:

£500 + £105,000 + £17,500 = £123,000

7)

Over 35	Under 35
2p	p

$2p + p = 990$

$3p = 990$

$p = \dfrac{990}{3}$

$p = 330$

Over 35 = 2 $x\ p$ = 2 x 330 = **660 people**.

Under 35 = 1 $x\ p$ = 1 x 330 = **330 people**.

8)

2009	2015	2018
10s	2s	s

$10s + 2s + s = 702$
$13s = 702$
$s = \dfrac{702}{13}$
$s = 54$

2009 = 10 $x\ s$ = 10 x 54 = **540 tonnes.**
2016 = 2 $x\ s$ = 2 x 54 = **108 tonnes.**
2018 = 1 $x\ s$ = 1 x 54 = **54 tonnes.**

9)

Plank A	Plank B	Plank C	Plank D
6l	2l	l	l

$6l + 2l + l + l = 60$
$10l = 60$
$l = \dfrac{60}{10}$
$l = 6$

Plank A = $6 \times l = 6 \times 6 =$ **36m.**
Plank B = $2 \times l = 2 \times 6 =$ **12m.**
Plank C = $1 \times l = 1 \times 6 =$ **6m.**
Plank D = $1 \times l = 1 \times 6 =$ **6m.**

10)

Furniture	Cutlery	Leaflets
4b	2b	b

$4b + 2b + b =$ £4,900
$7b =$ £4,900
$b = \dfrac{4,900}{7}$
$b = 700$

Furniture = $4 \times b = 4 \times 700 =$ **£2800**
Cutlery = $2 \times b = 2 \times 700 =$ **£1400**
Leaflets = $1 \times b = 1 \times 700 =$ **£700**

Answers – End of topic assessment

1) Money spent by Tiffany in total = Cost of stall hire + $\frac{81}{9}$ cost of box of contour kits

   $M = S + 9C$

2) Total money spent by Sohal = 0.6 x (Deposit + Estate agent fees)
   $T = 0.6(D + E)$
   Notes: In this question

3) Number of seeds left = (0.25 x Sunflower seeds) + (0.55 x Sweet pea seeds) + (0.80 x Primrose seeds)
   $L = 0.25Y + 0.55S + 0.80P$

4) Profit left = ((67 x Profit on each pair of boots) + (90 x Profit on each handbag)) - Cost of new stock
   $P = (67B + 90H) - S$

5) Area of a triangle = ½ x Base x Height
   $A = \frac{1}{2}(Y(4Y + 8))$
   $A = \frac{1}{2}(4Y^2 + 8Y)$
   $A = 2Y^2 + 4Y$

6) Perimeter = All sides added together
   $P = (5x + 2y) + (5x + 2y) + (x - y) + (x - y)$
   $P = 12x + 2y$

7) $z = \frac{x(y - x)}{2}$

   $z = \frac{20(60 - 20)}{2}$

   $z = \frac{20 \times 40}{2}$

   $z = \frac{800}{2}$

   $z = 400$

8) $j = (v + c)(v - c)$
   $j = (5 + 12)(5 - 12)$
   $j = 17 \times -7$
   $j = -119$

9) $i = \frac{b(bn)}{n}$

$i = \frac{2(2 \times 6)}{6}$

$i = \frac{24}{6}$

$i = 4$

10) $(2r + 4e) = v(r + 2e)$

$(18 + 8) = v(9 + 4)$

$26 = 13v$

$\frac{26}{13} = v$

$v = 2$

11) $d = \sqrt{t + r}$

$d = \sqrt{(9 + 16)}$

$d = \sqrt{25}$

$d = 5$

12) $d = 4a^2 + 2b - c$

$d = (4 \times 4^2) + (2 \times 6) - 7$

$d = (4 \times 16) + 12 - 7$

$d = 64 + 12 + 7$

$d = 69$

13)

a) $vf - g = h$

$vf = h + g$

$v = \frac{(h + g)}{f}$

b) $\frac{g}{v} - h = kl$

$\frac{g}{v} = kl + h$

$g = v(kl + h)$

$\frac{g}{kl + h} = v$

$v = \frac{g}{kl + h}$

c) $\sqrt{yv} = Q$

$yv = Q^2$

$v = \frac{Q^2}{y}$

d) $2h^2 + v = hy$
$v = hy - 2h^2$

e) $(h+v)^2 = z$
$h + v = \sqrt{z}$
$v = \sqrt{z} + h$

f) $g\sqrt{\dfrac{v}{h}} = j$
$\sqrt{\dfrac{v}{h}} = \dfrac{j}{g}$
$\dfrac{v}{h} = \left(\dfrac{j}{g}\right)^2$
$v = \left(\dfrac{j}{g}\right)^2 h$

14)
a) $3i + 4 = i + 13$
$3i - i = 13 - 4$
$2i = 9$
$i = \dfrac{9}{2}$
$i = 4.5$

b) $2i + 5 = 10$
$2i = 10 - 5$
$2i = 5$
$i = \dfrac{5}{2}$
$i = 2.5$

c) $3 + 6i = 6$
$6i = 6 - 3$
$6i = 3$
$i = \dfrac{3}{6}$
$i = \dfrac{1}{2}$

d) $2i + 11 = 17$
$2i = 17 - 11$
$2i = 6$
$i = \dfrac{6}{2}$
$i = 3$

e) $7 + 5i = 8i + 1$
$5i - 8i = 1 - 7$
$-3i = -6$
$i = \frac{-6}{-3}$
$i = 2$

f) $4i - 3 = 2i + 27$
$4i - 2i = 27 + 3$
$2i = 30$
$i = \frac{30}{2}$
$i = 15$

g) $\frac{10+2i}{4} = 7$
$10 + 2i = 7 \times 4$
$10 + 2i = 28$
$2i = 28 - 10$
$2i = 18$
$i = \frac{18}{2}$
$i = 9$

h) $3(2i + 4) = i - 13$
$6i + 12 = i - 13$
$6i - i = -13 - 12$
$5i = -25$
$i = \frac{-25}{5}$
$i = -5$

i) $i = \frac{9i - 15}{12}$
$12i = 9i - 15$
$12i - 9i = -15$
$3i = -15$
$i = \frac{-15}{3}$
$i = -5$

j) $3(2i - 1) + 2(i + 4) = 29$
$(6i - 3) + (2i + 8) = 29$
$6i - 3 + 2i + 8 = 29$
$8i = 24$
$i = \frac{24}{8}$
$i = 3$

15) $\frac{2}{5}h + 30 = 50 - \frac{3}{5}h$
$\frac{2}{5}h + \frac{3}{5}h = 50 - 30$
$h = 20$

16) $5(4v + 20) = -5v - 25$
$20v + 100 = -5v - 25$
$20v + 5v = -25 - 100$
$25v = -125$
$v = \frac{-125}{25}$
$v = -5$

17) $\frac{2}{5}q + 55 = 45 - \frac{3}{5}q$

$\frac{2}{5}q + \frac{3}{5}q = 45 - 55$

$q = -10$

18) $(n + 2) = 6(n - 2)$

$3n + 6 = 6n - 12$

$3n - 6n = -12 - 6$

$-3n = -18$

$n = \frac{-18}{-3}$

$n = 6$

Note: Here it is important that students remember that a negative number divided by another negative number gives a positive number.

19)

Symbol	Value
 ♥	10
 ☺	20
 ◇	12
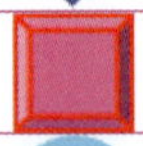 ▪	8
●	24

20) $\frac{(a-7)}{7} = 2$

$(a - 7) = 2 \times 7$

$a - 7 = 14$

$a = 14 + 7$

$a = 21$

21) *Sum of all angles in a triangle* $= 180°$

$(x + 60°) + (x + 20°) + 2x = 180°$

$4x + 80° = 180°$

$4x = 180° - 80°$

$4x = 100°$

$x = \frac{100°}{4}$

$x = 25°$

In order to find out the value of each of the angles A, B and C we must now substitute this value of x into each of the individual angle equations.

$A = x + 60°$

$A = 25° + 60°$

$A = 85°$

$B = x + 20°$

$B = 25° + 20°$

$B = 45°$

$C = 2x$

$C = 2 \times 25°$

$C = 50°$

22) *Sum of all angles in a trapezium* = 360°

$(x - 20°) + (x + 20°) + 90° + 90° = 360°$

$2x + 180° = 360°$

$2x = 360° - 180°$

$2x = 180°$

$x = \dfrac{180°}{2}$

$x = 90$.

Now substitute this value of x into eaxh of the individual angle equations to find their value

$A = (x - 20°)$

$A = 90° - 20°$

$A = 70°$

$B = (x + 20°)$

$B = 90° + 20°$

$B = 110°$

23)

Dinesh	Tamzin
4m	m

$4m + m = £20,000$
$5m = £20,000$
$m = \dfrac{£20,000}{5}$
$m = £4,000$

Now in order to calculate how much each of them contributed to the deposit we must substitute this value of m back into the equation.

$Dinesh = £m$
$Dinesh = £4,000$

$Tamzin = £4m$
$Tamzin = £4 \times 4,000$
$Tamzin = £16,000$

24)

Joginder	Susan	Mary
7.5c	c	2.5 c

Cakes baked by all three friends = 222

$7.5c + c + 2.5c = 220$

$11c = 220$

$c = \frac{220}{11}$

$c = 20$

Joginder = $7.5 \times c = 7.5 \times 20$ = **150 cakes.**

Susan = $1 \times c = 1 \times 20$ = **20 cakes.**

Mary = $2.5 \times c = 2.5 \times 20$ = **50 cakes.**

Printed in Great
Britain
by Amazon